NEW VANGUARD • 188

# GREAT LAKES
# WARSHIPS 1812–1815

**MARK LARDAS**                    ILLUSTRATED BY PAUL WRIGHT

First published in Great Britain in 2012 by Osprey Publishing,
Midland House, West Way, Botley, Oxford, OX2 0PH, UK
44–02 23rd St, Suite 219, Long Island City, NY 11101, USA

E-mail: info@ospreypublishing.com

Osprey Publishing is part of the Osprey Group

A CIP catalog record for this book is available from the British Library

Print ISBN: 978 1 84908 566 3
PDF e-book ISBN: 978 1 84908 565 6
EPUB e-book ISBN: 978 1 78096 048 7

Page layout by: Melissa orrom Swan, Oxford
Index by Margaret Vaudrey
Typeset in Sabon and Myriad Pro
Originated by PDQ Digital Media Solutions Ltd, Suffolk
Printed in China through Worldprint Ltd

12 13 14 15 16    10 9 8 7 6 5 4 3 2 1

Osprey Publishing is supporting the Woodland Trust, the UK's leading
woodland conservation charity, by funding the dedication of trees.

www.ospreypublishing.com

## AUTHOR'S ACKNOWLEDGMENT

I would like to thank Kevin Crisman, Associate Professor, Nautical
Archaeology Program and the Director, Center for Maritime Archaeology
and Conservation at Texas A&M University, for his assistance. He guided
me to a wealth of information on this topic. In addition, he made several
illustrations available to me. For those seeking to go deeper into the topic
of the warships of the inland lakes, I would recommend Kevin Crisman's
upcoming book. While this book is in the review phase at the time I write
these words, it is provisionally titled *Coffins of the Brave: The Nautical
Archaeology of the Naval War of 1812 on the Lakes.*

I would also like to thank two of Crisman's graduate students, Daniel Walker
and Erika Washburn, for making illustrations from their theses available
to me in this book. I also wish to thank Dan Thompson, model-maker,
and Bill Brodeur of Discovery Harbour, Penetanguishene, Ontario, Canada
(www.discoveryharbour.on.ca) for permission to use images included in
this book. In addition, thanks go to the Houston Maritime Museum and the
Gulf Coast Historic Ship Model Society for their help with my research. The
book is stronger for everyone's assistance, although any errors that may
remain are entirely my responsibility.

## AUTHOR'S DEDICATION

This book is dedicated to Kevin Crisman, a pioneer in lakes archeology,
and a man who defines the terms of gentleman and scholar.

## AUTHOR'S NOTE

The following abbreviations indicate the sources of the illustrations used
in this volume:

LOC – Library of Congress, Washington, DC

USN – US Navy

USNH&HC – US Navy History and Heritage Command, Washington, DC

USNA – US Naval Academy Collections

AC – Author's Collection

Other sources are listed in full.

# CONTENTS

# GREAT LAKES WARSHIPS 1812–1815

## INTRODUCTION

The hull of the *New Orleans* was a gaunt silhouette etched against the skyline. It had never been launched, and was still cradled on its building ways. Yet it was a ruin. That was unsurprising – the hull was nearly 70 years old. It had been constructed in the winter months of 1814 and 1815, and left incomplete. No further work was done, except to roof the hull over in an effort to preserve the ship for future use.

That need never came. By 1883, the ship was an anachronism. *New Orleans* was, as a ship-of-the-line, the class of warship that had decided the Battle of Trafalgar almost 80 years earlier. But *New Orleans* stood far from the saltwater oceans that were the normal habitat of that species. Rather, its building ways were on the shore of Lake Ontario, a freshwater sea 150 miles from the nearest ocean.

'Sea' is the right word to describe Lake Ontario. 'Lake' implies a smaller body of water, something that one could canoe across, and primarily useful for recreation. Yet Ontario, along with sister lakes Erie, Huron, Michigan, and Superior, were on a far larger scale, tens of thousands of square miles in area and hundreds of miles in length and width. Carved out by glaciers, the Great Lakes, along with their tributaries and a few smaller lakes, such as Lake Champlain downstream of Lake Ontario, formed part of the St Lawrence Watershed.

*New Orleans* was the largest ship in the US Navy when its construction began in 1814. Work on the ship-of-the-line ceased after peace in 1815. It remained incomplete on its building ways for nearly 70 years, before being disassembled in 1883. (USNH&C)

From the 1600s until the early 1800s, when the American railroad finally appeared, this waterway offered a highway into the heart of the North American continent, one along which goods and people could move. Movement was not effortless. Shallows, rapids, and falls interrupted free passage by water, requiring portaging. But those sections were typically short, and the size of the lakes offered unparalleled access to the continental interior. The lakes were so large that, except at choke points like the St Clair River linking Lakes Huron and Erie, access could not be dominated by shore batteries, certainly not by smoothbore artillery, whose 3-mile maximum range led to the initial definition of territorial waters. Even Lake Champlain, a 125-mile long slot, was 14 miles across at its widest point.

To control such sizable lakes and to ship goods across them required big ships, as large as the unfinished and now-useless ship-of-the-line on the banks of Lake Ontario. The Navy would sell its hulk and have it dismantled later that year. Yet for a brief three years, ships similar to it clashed on these waters in an effort to dominate them.

## DESIGN AND DEVELOPMENT

The Great Lakes offered naval architects unique advantages and challenges. For a start, the lakes are freshwater bodies. Freshwater has distinct maritime benefits. Ships on freshwater lakes need only a day's worth of drinking water – a bucket over the side allowed the supply to be refreshed. In the early 1800s, as long as you took the water from the lake itself, not from a harbor where ships moored, it was safe to drink. As late as the 1970s, freighters drew drinking

The St Lawrence Watershed, which included the Great Lakes and Lake Champlain, was the thoroughfare into the North American interior in 1812. (LOC)

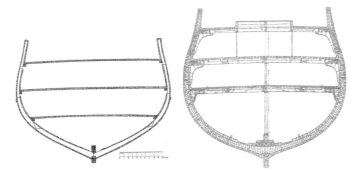

The difference in fullness and deadrise of ocean-going and lakes warships can be seen in this comparison between the cross-section of frigates *Princess Charlotte* (left) and *Constitution* (right). (*Princess Charlotte* line reprinted courtesy of Daniel Walker, *Constitution*, USN)

Modern replicas of HMS *Tecumseth* (left) and HMS *Bee* (right), schooners built for the Royal Navy on Lake Huron in 1816. *Tecumseth*, a warship, and *Bee* a transport, are representative of the vessels used on the upper lakes by the British. (Photo courtesy of Discovery Harbour, Penetanguishene, Ontario, Canada. Web: www.discoveryharbour.on.ca)

water, untreated, from Lake Superior. Lacking the necessity to store large quantities of barreled drinking water, storage requirements were reduced.

Freshwater also kills teredo worms – shipworms – which bored through the wooden hulls of ocean-going ships. Such vessels were protected from shipworm by lining the underwater hull with copper plates, but copper-bottoming a ship was expensive, and unnecessary on the lakes. Seawater is also 3 percent denser than freshwater. A ship drawing 12ft of water off Cape Cod had a draft of 12ft 4in on Lake Ontario.

On the debit side, lakes warships faced greater challenges in terms of stability. Stability is a function of a ship's center of gravity – the higher the center of gravity, the less stable a ship becomes. Ninteenth-century ocean-going vessels had low centers of gravity by virtue of copper plating on the bottom of the hull, plus the storage of large amounts of food and water in the lower hold. A lakes warship did not require the copper plating, nor the extensive stores of food and water (the ships were never more than two days from port), but without them the ship's center of gravity was much higher. Placing heavy guns on a ship's deck or even adding solid bulwarks exacerbated the problem.

The stability problem was further exacerbated because of a desire for speed. While the lakes were big, virtually any destination within one lake could be reached in a couple of days, even sailing at 5mph (4.3 knots). (Statute miles were customarily used by lakes mariners.) But ships with a good turn of speed, say 13¾mph (12 knots) could complete a typical voyage between sunrise and sunset, thereby simplifying watch-keeping and reducing the need for crew accommodations while increasing cargo space.

Speed was achieved by building hulls with high deadrise. Deadrise is the angle of the hull measured from the keel to its widest beam. Flat-bottomed hulls have no deadrise, whereas "V"-shaped hulls have high deadrise. All other factors being equal in two hulls of the same volume, the hull with the higher deadrise will be faster. High deadrise reduces the volume in the lower part of the hull. This reduces the fullness of the hull, and raises the center of gravity. Sailing ships with low deadrise had greater endurance than ships with high deadrise. They could also carry more stores, limiting the deadrise on ocean-going vessels. But endurance was less important than speed on the lakes, so shipwrights used higher deadrise – further raising the center of gravity.

Another consideration in ship design and rig was due to the geography of the lakes. While the lakes were deep – the average depth of the shallowest, Lake Erie, was 62ft – the harbors and coastlines could be quite shallow. At the start of the 19th century, dredging lay in the future, so lakes ships were built to a shallower draft than their ocean-going counterparts. Since much of the sailing these ships did was along coastlines, fore-and-aft rigs were favored over square rigs for mercantile vessels, although ships built as warships used brig or ship rigs.

In terms of ship construction the lakes offered abundant timber. Oak for hulls, elm for keels, and pine for masts were plentiful. Much of it was timber from fully mature trees, of a size not seen in Europe since the Vikings. Primitive transportation often made getting the timber to a yard a challenge, but if you wanted to build a small ship – 300 tons or less, you could simply put your building ways close to your sources of wood.

Amherstburg on the Detroit River was the main British naval shipyard for Lake Erie and the upper lakes. Its loss in 1813, combined with the American victory at Put-in-Bay, guaranteed US control of Lake Erie. (AC)

## Pre-War Warship Construction

Naval battles were fought on the inland lakes prior to the War of 1812, most notably on Lake Champlain during the American Revolution. Yet during the first decade of the 19th century, only a handful of warships were built, and were intended more for law enforcement than projecting naval power. Each nation had to maintain three sets of ships, one each on Lake Ontario, Lake Champlain, and Lake Erie, as these lakes were physically separated. Ships based on Lake Erie, however, could sail into Lake Huron and from there into Georgian Bay or Lake Michigan. Yet by 1812, although the Great Lakes area was still largely frontier – for both Great Britain and the United States – it was important.

Britain had a larger naval presence on the lakes than the United States with its penurious federal government. British warships there belonged to the Provincial Marine rather than the Royal Navy. They were an adjunct of the British Army, and provided a military transport service. Their personnel were not necessarily members of the Royal Navy; although its officers were frequently seconded from the Royal Navy, many enlisted members were recruited locally, in the same way as those recruited for the customs service cutters in Britain.

Britain created small naval establishments on both Lake Ontario and Lake Erie prior to the war: Kingston and York on Lake Ontario, and Amherstburg on the Detroit River, the major inlet of Lake Erie. During the American Revolution, Britain used Isle aux Noix on the Richelieu River as their shipyard for Lake Champlain, but shut down this station shortly after the war ended.

The Provincial Marine's dockyard and offices at Kingston were established in 1789. York was added in the mid 1790s. Both dockyards built Provincial Marine ships, launching a dozen ships between them prior to the war of 1812. The Lake Erie station at Amherstburg opened in 1796, after Britain turned over its previous station at Detroit to the United States. By 1812, Amherstburg had built four warships for the Provincial Marine.

Most of the British vessels were small schooners, intended to help the government maintain communications or enforce customs laws. Generally only three or four ships were kept in service on Lake Ontario, and one or two on Lake Erie. The service life of pre-war vessels averaged eight years. Only five were usable when war was declared in June 1812 – *Duke of Gloucester*, *Earl of Moira*, and *Royal George* on Lake Ontario, and *General Hunter* and *Queen Charlotte* on Lake Erie. *Gloucester* was a six-gun schooner; *General*

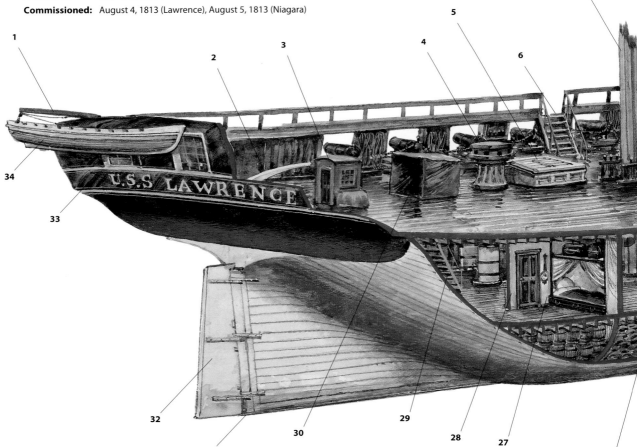

# A LAWRENCE AND NIAGARA (BRIGS-OF-WAR)

These brigs were built and designed by Noah and Adam Brown, with construction supervised by Daniel Dobbins. Both were at the Battle of Lake Erie, with *Lawrence*, seen here, serving as the American flagship. After *Lawrence* was disabled, Perry transferred to *Niagara* and used the previously unengaged ship to win the battle.

*Lawrence* was sunk for preservation in Misery Bay (near Erie, Pennsylvania) after the end of the war in 1815. In 1875 it was raised for use as a display at the 1876 US Centennial Exhibition in Philadelphia, Pennsylvania. Cut into sections, it was transported by rail to Philadelphia where it was reassembled. The pavilion in which it was displayed caught fire, and the ship was destroyed in the subsequent blaze.

*Niagara* served as a receiving ship following the war's end. In 1820 it also was sunk for preservation next to *Lawrence*. *Niagara*'s hull was raised in 1913 and the ship was partially restored for the centennial anniversary of the Battle of Lake Erie. After touring Lakes Erie, Huron, and Michigan in 1913, the ship was returned to Erie, Pennsylvania, and placed on display out of the water. The ship deteriorated, and in 1929 ownership was transferred to a commission intended to restore the ship. Reconstruction, slowed by the Great Depression, was completed in the 1960s. In 1986 the hull was examined and found badly decayed. *Niagara* was dismantled and a new *Niagara* built from the remaining usable timbers of the original ship. The rebuilt ship, considered by some a replica, was launched in 1988. It is currently on display at Erie, Pennsylvania.

## Technical Data

| | |
|---|---|
| **Dimensions:** | LBP: 110', Breadth: 30', Depth of Hold: 9', Draft 10' 6" |
| **Displacement:** | 493 tons |
| **Complement:** | 135 |
| **Armament:** | 18 x 32lb carronades, 2 x 12lb long guns |
| **Built:** | Erie, Pennsylvania |
| **Laid Down:** | March 1813 (both) |
| **Launched:** | May 1813 (both) |
| **Commissioned:** | August 4, 1813 (Lawrence), August 5, 1813 (Niagara) |

**Key**

1. Stern davit
2. Tiller
3. Captain's cabin skylight
4. Capstan
5. Wardroom skylight
6. Entryway
7. Mainmast
8. Launch
9. 32lb carronade
10. Fore hatch
11. Galley smokestack
12. 12lb long gun
13. Foremast
14. Bowsprit
15. Jib boom
16. Martingale
17. Cathead
18. Riding bitts
19. Bosun's store
20. Galley
21. Sail locker
22. Crew berthing
23. Main hatch and ladder
24. Main fife rails
25. Shot locker
26. Cock pit
27. Officers' cabin
28. Wardroom
29. After ladder
30. After companionway
31. Stern post
32. Rudder
33. Transom
34. Gig

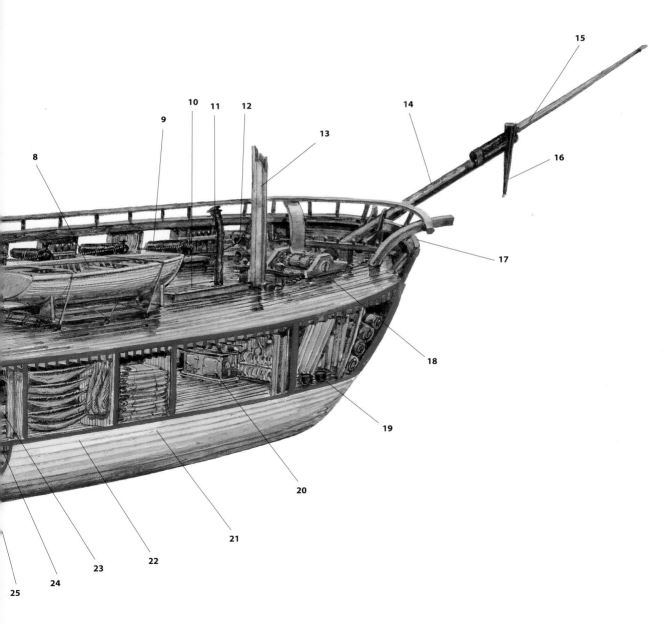

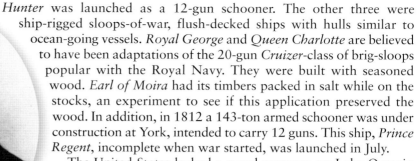

Henry Eckford had been a shipbuilder in New York City, when Chauncey hired him to oversee construction of the lakes fleets. He not only designed many of the ships, he also built the shipyard at Sackett's Harbor. (USNH&HC)

*Hunter* was launched as a 12-gun schooner. The other three were ship-rigged sloops-of-war, flush-decked ships with hulls similar to ocean-going vessels. *Royal George* and *Queen Charlotte* are believed to have been adaptations of the 20-gun *Cruiser*-class of brig-sloops popular with the Royal Navy. They were built with seasoned wood. *Earl of Moira* had its timbers packed in salt while on the stocks, an experiment to see if this application preserved the wood. In addition, in 1812 a 143-ton armed schooner was under construction at York, intended to carry 12 guns. This ship, *Prince Regent*, incomplete when war started, was launched in July.

The United States lacked a naval presence on Lake Ontario until 1807, when the Jefferson Administration ordered a gunboat built on that lake to enforce the recently passed Embargo Act, which barred US merchant vessels from carrying cargoes to foreign countries. While aimed at ocean-going commerce, it also affected trade on the lakes, permitting American ships to carry goods between Oswego and Niagara, but not Oswego and Kingston.

The Navy contracted construction of the vessel to Henry Eckford, a shipbuilder in New York City. Then 33 years old, Eckford was a partner at Bergh & Eckford, a yard with a long history of building ships for the US Navy. Eckford, the junior partner, was sent to Lake Ontario in 1808 to establish a yard and construct the gunboat.

Eckford's ship was much different to the oared gunboat originally envisioned. Built at Oswego, and christened *Oneida*, it more closely resembled the sea-going brig-sloops created for the US Navy than a Jeffersonian gunboat. Intended to carry 16 carriage-mounted broadside guns and a long 32lb gun on a pivot in the bow, it was built with a lofty brig rig. The 32-pdr was never mounted. Instead of a gunboat, the resulting ship was a flush-deck, brig-rigged sloop-of-war. As with *Earl of Moira*, the timbers were packed in salt during construction for preservation.

The US Navy had no presence on Lake Erie prior to 1812. The only armed American ship there was *Adams*, a 125-ton brig operated by the US Army. It carried six small guns, and carried supplies for Army garrisons at Detroit and Michilimackinac. Minor shipyards dotted the American side of the upper lakes, but only at Detroit, where the Provincial Marine station had previously been located, had warships been built.

## Wartime Shipbuilding by the United States

The major American aim within the War of 1812 was to capture Canada. When the war began that June, Britain had naval superiority on both Lake Ontario and on Lake Erie and the upper lakes. Only on Lake Champlain did the United States have parity, because neither nation had warships on that lake when the war began. Regardless, the United States expected Canada to quickly fall. Instead, by August most of the Michigan Territory was controlled by Britain. Just regaining the lost territory – much less capturing Upper Canada (today's Ontario) – required control of the lakes.

Isaac Chauncey was given command of American naval forces on the lakes, with authority to purchase, hire, and build whatever was required for naval supremacy. He initially reinforced his fleet by purchasing and arming merchant ships on the lakes, but these proved inadequate. Lakes trading vessels were small – between 80 and 110 tons displacement. They could only carry a handful of guns, although this limitation was mitigated to some extent by placing the guns on pivot mounts that allowed one gun to fire on either side. Arming small merchant vessels also created stability problems, making the ships dangerous to operate. Purpose-built warships were needed.

Chauncey chose Sackett's Harbor near Lake Ontario's eastern end as the site of a naval base and shipyard, and put Henry Eckford in charge of lakes shipbuilding, hiring 100 shipwrights from New York City and moving materials from downstate New York via a river network. Eckford acted swiftly. By early September 1812, Eckford laid the keel for the first warship in the Sackett's Harbor yard (the site had been an open field a month earlier) – a 24-gun sloop-of-war. The hull was completed in 45 days, and launched on November 26. It was the first of many examples of lightning-fast shipbuilding by Henry Eckford.

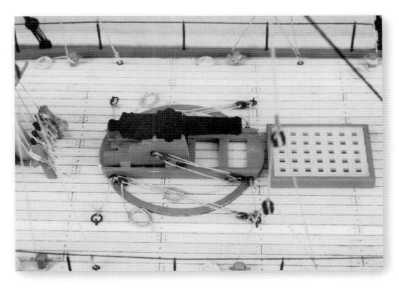

The pivot mount allowed a gun to be pointed in any direction. It allowed use of larger guns, and allowed a single gun to be fired on both broadsides. (Courtesy of Dan Thompson)

Meanwhile, efforts to create a Lake Erie shipyard had started. A merchant master from that lake, Daniel Dobbins, went to Washington, DC, to report on conditions on the upper lakes. He was given a US Navy Master's warrant, and the job of creating a naval yard near Erie, Pennsylvania, and building four gunboats on it. By December, Dobbins had erected a work shed and blacksmith's shop across Presque Isle Bay, opposite Erie, had hired a local shipbuilder, and started work on two small gunboats. These became the schooners *Porcupine* and *Tigress*, each mounting a 32lb long gun on a bow-mounted pivot.

*Madison*, *Porcupine*, and *Tigress* were soon followed by vessels of ever-increasing size. On Lake Ontario, Eckford laid down a new warship, *General Pike*, on April 9, 1813. While rated as a sloop-of-war, it was a miniature frigate, mounting 26 x 24lb long guns. The ship was launched 64 days later – despite an interruption to repair fire damage when the British raided Sackett's Harbor. *General Pike* was followed by *Sylph*, started in July and launched 23 days later. Initially rigged as a schooner, *Sylph* mounted 18 guns, and was later re-rigged as a brig.

On Lake Erie, four more ships rose on the building stocks in 1813 – two schooners, *Scorpion* and *Ariel*, and two 500-ton brigs, *Lawrence* and *Niagara*. These ships were designed by New York City shipbuilders Noah and Adam Brown. Chauncey hired the brothers and sent them to Presque Isle early in 1813. Like Eckford, they showed a real ability to build first-rate ships quickly. Arriving in March, with 200 men, the Browns laid down four warships and launched the hulls by the end of May. The schooners were in service by July and the brigs were commissioned in the first week of August – the delay in the brig commissioning was caused by the late arrival of the guns and related fittings.

The pace of shipbuilding increased in 1814. Eckford supervised construction of two large brigs at Sackett's Harbor; *Jefferson* and *Jones*. They were based on the design of the ship-rigged *Peacock*-class sloops-of-war, although the lakes adaptations were 2ft 6in longer than the *Peacock*. Both

Daniel Dobbins was a merchant master in the Northwest Territories before the War of 1812. In late 1812 he was sent to Lake Erie with instructions to build a naval yard and warships for the upper lakes. He laid the foundations for Perry's fleet. (AC)

were laid down and launched in two months, and each carried a battery of 20 heavy guns. Bigger ships followed. Three frigates were laid down over the spring and summer of 1814. Eckford designed and built a 62-gun frigate, *Superior*, and a smaller 42-gun frigate, *Mohawk*. *Superior* was laid down in February and launched in May. *Mohawk* was completed even more quickly; laid down in May, it was launched in June.

The Brown brothers transferred east from Lake Erie in early 1814. Initially they were sent to Lake Champlain, where the Navy had a shipyard at Vergennes, Vermont, that formed a response to British shipbuilding at Isle aux Noix. Over a six-month period, the Browns built three large warships and six large oared galleys. The warships were the sloop-of-war *Saratoga* (26 guns), schooner *Ticonderoga* (17 guns), and brig *Eagle* (20 guns). *Ticonderoga* was converted from the unfinished hull of a merchant steamboat being built at Vergennes. The engines were removed and the ship completed as a schooner. *Saratoga* and *Eagle* were conventional warships, but both were completed with the Browns' usual speed. *Saratoga* was launched 40 days after its construction began and *Eagle* after 31 days.

The Browns then moved to Sackett's Harbor, where they designed and supervised the construction of three more ships – the third Lake Ontario frigate (larger than *Superior* and named *Plattsburg*) and two ships-of-the-line. The ships-of-the-line, *New Orleans* and *Chippewa*, were built in response to a British ship-of-the-line launched that autumn. The American vessels each could carry nearly 90 x 32lb guns. Construction was completed through the upper gun deck before being suspended over winter. As the war ended early in 1815, none of the three ships were finished, remaining on the building ways to meet future needs.

The rapid construction of these warships was made possible through a number of short-cuts. Green, rather than seasoned, wood was used. Local timber was cut, and cut on the basis of what approximated the right shape rather than what type of wood was traditionally used. *Eagle*'s keel used a mixture of

## B  CONSTRUCTION OF A LAKES WARSHIP

One of the most remarkable aspects of the naval war on the lakes was the speed with which both sides built their ships. The territory around the Great Lakes then was still frontier in both the United States and Canada. While construction was supervised by skilled shipwrights, trained labor was often in short supply, seasoned timber was unavailable, and iron fittings had to be shipped long distances to the construction sites. Gangs of carpenters sent from coastal cities did the skilled work, while locally recruited residents provided the muscle required to raise the frames into place.

The building slip was usually a patch of ground hacked out of the local countryside on the waterfront. Timber was taken from what trees grew near at hand. Less emphasis was placed on the type of wood than on its shape. Maple, oak, and pine might be mixed together in the hull based on availability and size. Frequently, especially in 1813 and 1814 when construction was at its most frantic, unseasoned, green timber was used, moved to the construction yard within hours of having been felled, and shaped as it arrived.

To save time, and simplify building, wartime construction often used shortcuts that would have been considered unacceptable under normal conditions. Knees – curved pieces of wood used to join the deck beams to the hull frames – were often omitted. It took too long to find crotch timber (formed where the tree trunk branched off) and then to cut it to shape. Instead, the deck beams were clamped to frames with timbers running longitudinally along the hull, reinforced with blocks of wood. The ships were crude and subject to rot. Yet they served well enough to fight the one decisive battle for which they were required.

maple and oak, and its frames were made from a bewildering assortment of non-traditional woods – white ash, spruce, elm, pine, and chestnut – in addition to the more usual oak. In addition, these ships were built without knees – curved timbers used to anchor deck beams to the frames. Constructing knees was time-consuming and finding appropriately shaped timbers difficult. Instead, the beams were clamped to the frames. This took less time, but produced a hull that wore out more quickly, as did building with unseasoned wood. As Oliver Perry shrewdly observed: "They are only required for one battle; if we win, that is all that will be wanted of them."

Noah and Adam Brown were well-known New York shipbuilders before being hired to assist Eckford in the inland lakes. Among the best-known ships built by the Browns prior to moving to the lakes was the privateer *Prince de Neufchateau*, shown above. (Author photo – Houston Maritime Museum)

## Wartime Shipbuilding by Great Britain

Despite the British advantages in shipbuilding facilities at the start of the War of 1812, the Provincial Marine launched no new ships during the first year of the war. Instead, British shipwrights concentrated on refitting existing ships. *Governor Simcoe*, a schooner built for Upper Canada's civil government, was rebuilt as a warship. The ship emerged from the dockyard as the 12-gun *Sir Sydney Smith*. Not until autumn, when Provincial Marine officials became alarmed at the reports of American shipbuilding on Lake Ontario, was a serious shipbuilding program undertaken by the British.

Two sloops-of-war were laid down that autumn – *Sir George Prevost* at Kingston and *Sir Isaac Brock* at York. Each displaced more than 400 tons, the largest ships yet started on the Great Lakes. Construction proceeded slowly. The Kingston ship was not launched until late April 1813 (when it was renamed *Wolfe*). Work on *Brock* moved at a more desultory pace. It was burned on the stocks in late May, when Chauncey's squadron raided York. Even then, its hull, started six months earlier, was incomplete.

The pace of shipbuilding picked up after *Wolfe*'s launch, when the Royal Navy took over the Provincial Marine. To counter the ships that Dobbins and the Browns were building at Presque Isle, a new ship-rigged sloop-of-war was started at Amherstburg. Adapted from the plans used for *Wolfe* and *Brock*, this ship, named *Detroit*, was launched in July 1813. On Lake Ontario work began on a new brig at Kingston. Named *Lord Melville*, this 186-ton warship was launched in July, adding another 14 guns to the Lake Ontario squadron.

By July, Captain Sir James L. Yeo, who had taken command of naval forces on the inland lakes, decided that British domination of these waters required larger warships. By October two frigates were being built at Kingston. The larger, a 56-gun frigate christened *Prince Regent*, was a lakes adaptation of *Leander*-class frigates that Britain had built in response to America's 1812 frigate victories. Smaller than the 1,573-ton *Leander* vessels at 1,293 tons, *Prince Regent* carried almost as heavy a battery, weighing 856lb. *Princess Charlotte* was smaller – comparable to the standard ocean-going 38-gun heavy frigate, but armed with a main battery of 24lb long guns. Both were built with extreme deadrise – 20 degrees for *Prince Regent* and 30 degrees for *Princess Charlotte*. Design of both frigates appears to have been done locally, with Patrick Fleming, a shipbuilder from Quebec, designing and overseeing construction of *Prince Regent* and George Record, the master shipwright at Kingston, designing and building *Princess Charlotte*.

While *Prince Regent*'s keel was laid in August 1813, the ship was not launched until April 15, 1814. Construction stalled due to a shortage of both materials and shipwrights, and it was not until ship fittings and a new draft of workers were sent from Quebec over the winter that the two ships could be completed. Commissioned in May, the two frigates tipped the balance on Lake Ontario until the American frigates appeared. The British anticipated Yankee

escalation, however, and in April 1814 the keel was laid for a ship-of-the-line.

*Duke of Gloucester* was typical of the small warships the Provincial Marine used prior to the War of 1812. Briefly used in 1812, it was unseaworthy by 1813. (AC)

Designed by William Bell, the ship, *St Lawrence*, was the biggest warship launched on the inland lakes, it mounted 104 guns on three decks. In many ways it was an extreme example of a lakes warship, with storage space and crew accommodations traded for the heaviest possible battery. When launched on October 9, 1814, it gave Britain command of Lake Ontario. Keels for two slightly smaller ships-of-the-line, *Wolfe* and *Canada*, were also laid down in late 1814. Each was intended to carry more guns than *St Lawrence*, 112 each, despite displacing 150 tons less. Construction was suspended following peace in 1815.

Britain expanded its shipbuilding efforts beyond Lake Ontario in 1814. On Lake Champlain, where the British previously used gunboats and captured prizes, they re-established a shipyard at Isle aux Noix. In addition to launching a number of rowed galleys, mounting large bow- or stern-mounted guns, in April the shipyard launched a 16-gun brig-sloop christened *Linnet*, and in response to American shipbuilding at Vergennes, a frigate was hastily built during the summer. Launched in August, its design reached an optimal speed of construction. The hull was described as "barge-like," and it was assembled from whatever timber was immediately at hand. *Confiance*, as the vessel was named, was launched in August, and sent into battle in September, with shipwrights aboard still finishing its outfitting.

James Yeo was sent from England to command the Royal Navy on the inland lakes. As with his American opposite number, he was a cautious commander, unwilling to fight without a substantial advantage. (AC)

Following the naval loss at Put-in-Bay on Lake Erie and the subsequent abandonment of Amherstburg in September 1813, Britain lost its major shipyard on the upper lakes. In 1814 a new shipyard was established at Penetanguishene in Georgian Bay, an inlet of Lake Huron. Plans were laid to build at least two frigates there, but the remote location slowed work on construction of the yard itself. Eventually, after the war's end, the facility built several armed schooners, but plans for constructing larger warships were shelved.

While – except at Lake Champlain – the British tended to use more traditional shipbuilding woods on their vessels' construction than their American counterparts, they did use several other time-saving construction techniques. These included omitting hanging knees, using simplified framing, and reducing notching of timbers. Iron nails were also used rather than wooden treenails or copper bolts. As with their American counterparts, British shipwrights realized their ships would probably fight but one battle.

Isle aux Noix was an island on the Richelieu River. Fortified during the American Revolution, its facilities had closed prior to the War of 1812. It was reopened to support British operations on Lake Champlain. The Royal Navy shipyard opened there in 1813. (AC)

## Prefabricated Warships

The most unusual program to provide warships for the inland lakes originated in Britain. Following the defeat of British forces on Lake Erie in September 1813, several proposals were raised to build the components for lakes warships in Britain and send the components, unassembled, to North America. From Quebec, parts would be shipped overland to yards on the inland lakes for completion.

Prefabrication – building the frames and other structural members in Britain – had several advantages. By late 1813, Britain had a surplus of building facilities and skilled shipwrights in its home waters, and stocks of seasoned timbers suitable for ship construction. All were in short supply in Upper Canada, the seat of the war. Sending 1:1-scale wooden ship kits to Canada leveraged Britain's strengths, and the prefabricated ships could be knocked together by semi-skilled builders in North America.

By December 1813, the Admiralty authorized construction of a 38-gun frigate "kit" in Britain for Lake Ontario. A second frigate and two brigs were added in January. The lines of the frigates, drafted for the Admiralty Board, were similar to conventional ocean-going British frigates of the period, with fuller hulls and less deadrise than the lakes frigates. Less is known of the brig sloops, but they were probably similar to the *Cruizer*-class brigs then popular with the Admiralty.

Construction of the frames for frigates *Psyche* and *Prompte*, and brigs *Goshawk* and *Colibri*, began in the Chatham dockyard in mid January 1814. Complete by the end of February, the frames were marked and loaded onto transports, along with the fittings and equipment necessary to complete them, in March. By July, the transports carrying the ships began arriving in North America.

The plan had been inadequately coordinated with those running the war in Canada. Sir George Prevost, commander-in-chief of British forces in North America, first learned of the forthcoming ships in April, after they had been loaded for shipment. Since three indigenous large warships were already under construction (and delayed by lack of manpower and materials), the reactions of the shipwrights on Lake Ontario were less positive than the Admiralty might have expected. By the time Yeo's response reached London, the ships were already en route. Their arrival was accompanied by positive orders to finish them, and (more welcome) 900 Royal Navy personnel to man the vessels.

The frames were unloaded at Montreal, where they initially remained. No means to transport them further inland existed. Then a transport carrying components was taken by an American privateer in September 1814. Thirty guns and a quantity of stores intended for the ships were lost.

Only one of the ships was completed. Frames for *Psyche* were slowly brought to Kingston over the late summer and early autumn of 1814. With the launch of *St Lawrence*, space was available for construction, and *Psyche*'s keel was laid on October 31. Thomas Strickland oversaw construction of the frigate, modifying it on the stocks so that it could carry 56 guns. *Psyche* was launched on December 25, 1814 – the last major lakes warship of the War of 1812.

## OPERATIONAL HISTORY

When the War of 1812 started in mid June 1812, the United States planned to seize Canada. The inland lakes were seen in terms of highways and supply lines for the invading American militia armies. The United States regarded the few armed ships they then had on the lakes as tools for customs enforcement, rather than control of the waters.

British efforts to build ships in England and ship them disassembled to North America were mocked in this American political cartoon, after a US privateer captured one of the transports carrying equipment for the prefabricated ships. (LOC)

George Prevost initially planned to stand on the defensive, despite his maritime superiority. He believed that raiding the United States, especially New York and New England, would increase American enthusiasm for a war. Regardless, America invaded Upper Canada, and the British counterattacked. The battle for Upper Canada became a naval war as much as a land war. Or rather, it became three naval wars: operations on Lake Ontario, Lake Erie, and Lake Champlain were fundamentally independent.

### Lake Ontario

When the war started, Britain possessed four warships – two sloops-of-war, *Earl of Moira* and *Royal George*, and two schooners, the elderly *Duke of Gloucester* and just-launched *Prince Regent*. The Provincial Marine outnumbered the US Navy, which consisted of *Oneida*, commanded by Lieutenant Melancthon Woolsey, the senior US naval officer on Lake Ontario. Regardless of the disparity, the Provincial Marine initially limited its activities to transport duties. It did attempt to recover a British merchant vessel seized by Woolsey at Sackett's Harbor, took a pair of small American merchant vessels at Charlotte, New York, and briefly blockaded Ogdensburg on the Niagara River.

Isaac Chauncey was an outstanding administrator, and an excellent organizer. He was also too cautious to risk his ships in combat, unless he had a numeric advantage. (AC)

The United States accomplished little more than the Provincial Marine in 1812, due to its meager resources. In September, the Secretary of the Navy, Paul Hamilton, ordered Captain Isaac Chauncey to the lakes to create an island navy. Chauncey, then commanding the New York Navy Yard, was told to take the crew of the frigate *John Adams*, and to buy or build whatever Chauncey required for his fleet. Chauncey, an excellent administrator and organizer, soon created a force superior to the Provincial Marine.

Chauncey converted nine small schooners into warships by fitting bulwarks to the open-sided vessels and adding guns – typically one or two large pivot-mounted guns, although four vessels also had carriage-mounted broadside guns. Overcoming difficulties – cannon, cordage, and supplies had to reach Lake Ontario from lower New York via a network of

Chauncey's maritime superiority over the British in early spring 1813 allowed him to project power through amphibious landings. He is shown here landing at Fort George. *Madison* is the ship-rigged vessel in the center foreground, while *Oneida* is to its right. (USNH&HC)

rivers and portages – the ships were converted and manned by November. Chauncey took his fleet out on November 10. Over three days it caught *Royal George*, *Governor Simcoe*, and *Earl of Moira* individually as they approached Kingston, and chased each into the harbor. Chauncey failed to capture these three ships, but *Governor Simcoe* was badly damaged after it grounded while entering Kingston. Chauncey also burned one British merchantman, and captured two others, which were added to his force as *Asp* and *Scorpion*.

Over the winter of 1812/13, Chauncey had two ship-rigged sloops-of-war and two armed schooners put into production at Sackett's Harbor. The British converted *Governor Simcoe* into a warship, and began work on a brig-of-war at Kingston, and ship-rigged sloops-of-war at both Kingston and York.

The United States won the first round of the building war, launching the 24-gun *Madison* and schooner *Lady of the Lake* in April 1813. Using this added strength, Chauncey took *Madison*, *Oneida*, his armed schooners, and 1,700 soldiers commanded by Zebulon Pike across Lake Ontario to York. Covered by the navy's guns and outnumbering the British garrison, Pike's soldiers landed at York on April 27, capturing the shipyard. The British burned the sloop-of-war *Sir Isaac Brock*, then under construction, and fired the magazine before withdrawing. The explosion caused heavy American casualties, killing Pike. Chauncey's squadron stripped York of guns and naval supplies before withdrawing and carried off the old *Gloucester*. Renamed *York*, it spent the war as a powder hulk at Sackett's Harbor.

In May, Chauncey launched another raid, this time at Niagara. On May 27, his squadron supported an assault on Fort George, in coordination with a US Army invasion across the Niagara River. Chauncey's force successfully took Fort George, but the American army was repulsed at Queenston. Then he received word that his Sackett's Harbor base was under attack.

Reacting to the crisis on the lakes, Admiral John Warren, commanding the Royal Navy's North American Station, sent Commander Robert Barclay to Lake Ontario. The Admiralty dispatched Captain Sir James L. Yeo with 465 Royal Navy officers and men from England. Barclay reached Kingston days after the April 25 launch of the Kingston sloop-of-war, *Sir George Prevost*. The Provincial Marine was dissolved, with its ships taken over by the Royal Navy. Yeo arrived at Kingston on May 15 with a commodore's pendant. Superseding Barclay, Yeo sent him to command the Lake Erie squadron.

Yeo soon took the offensive. On May 27, he sailed from Kingston with *Wolfe* (formerly *Sir George Prevost*), *Royal George*, *Earl of Moira*, *Lord Beresford* (formerly the schooner *Prince Regent*), and *Sir Sidney Smith* (converted from *Governor Simcoe*) and 800 troops led by Governor Prevost. The British landed on May 29, and almost captured the naval base. Light winds kept Yeo's ships from supporting the army's attack on Fort Tompkins, guarding the yard. Prevost suspended the attack when the sloop-of-war under construction at the naval yard appeared to be burning, and the British withdrew back to Kingston.

Chauncey rushed back to Sackett's Harbor. He found it still intact. Even the sloop-of-war, accidentally set on fire during the raid, was still there, albeit fire-damaged. Chauncey decided that Yeo's *Wolfe* had swung the balance back in Britain's favor. He therefore chose to remain in harbor until his sloop-of-war was completed. *General Pike* – as the ship was christened – was not commissioned until late July. By then the brig *Lord Melville* had joined Yeo. Over August and September 1813, Yeo and Chauncey battled to control Lake Ontario.

The two fleets sighted each other off Niagara on August 7, but did not engage. That night a violent storm hit, sinking two of Chauncey's schooners – *Hamilton* and *Scourge*. On August 10, Chauncey lured Yeo into combat, by using his schooners as bait. When the schooners fell back to join Chauncey's main battle line, two – *Growler* and *Julia* – turned the wrong way, and were isolated. Yeo snapped them up. In three days, Chauncey lost four ships. Yeo initially used the prize schooners as warships, but soon converted them into unarmed transports.

The British attack on Sackett's Harbor was repulsed by a combination of its fortifications and the navy defenders around the port.

Chauncey went after Yeo again in September. He had been reinforced by the schooner *Sylph*. The two fleets met again twice in September, the first on September 11, when Chauncey found Yeo off the Genesee River in calm waters, and the second on September 28, south of York in gale conditions. Both battles were indecisive. *Pike* managed to dismast *Wolfe* on September 28, but a gun burst on *Pike*, and *Royal George*'s support helped *Wolfe* escape. Little further action occurred in 1813, although in October, Chauncey captured five British transports in an inadequately guarded convoy. The prizes included the ships he lost on August 10 – *Growler* and *Julia*.

The main lesson both sides learned in 1813 was that broadside weight mattered. Both sides began building large sloops-of-war, frigates, and eventually, ships-of-the-line. Ignored was the lesson of Lake Erie – aggressiveness also matters. Throughout 1814, neither fleet would come out when its commander perceived it was inferior.

The battle between Chauncey and Yeo on September 11, 1813, lasted 3 hours and 40 minutes. Fought in light airs, it was indecisive. This drawing was made by Midshipman Peter Spicer. During this battle he was aboard USS *Sylph*, the second ship from the right in the upper line. (USNH&HC)

In 1814, the British finished frigates *Prince Regent* and *Princess Charlotte* before the American frigates. To confuse Chauncey, Yeo also renamed his existing ships. *Royal George* became *Niagara* and *Earl of Moira* the *Charwell*, *Lord Beresford* was renamed *Netley*, *Sir Sidney Smith* rechristened *Magnet*, *Wolfe* became *Montreal* and *Lord Melville*, *Star*. In early May Yeo crossed Lake Ontario, landing at Oswego on May 5 for a two-day raid. Yeo got little besides some stores, but Chauncey, feeling outnumbered, did not oppose the raid. In mid May Yeo blockaded Sackett's Harbor for two weeks.

Fearing the balance tipping against him as the American frigates neared completion, Yeo withdrew to Kingston at the end of May to await completion of his ship-of-the-line.

July and August were Chauncey's months to rule Lake Ontario. His only success occurred on August 5, when his ships trapped *Magnet*, which was blown up to prevent capture. In September, Yeo's ship-of-the-line, *St Lawrence*, was launched. Chauncey again withdrew behind his Sackett's Harbor defenses to await 1815 and his own reinforcement by two ships-of-the-line and another large frigate. The war on Lake Ontario ended as it began – in stalemate.

The US Army brig *Adams* was captured by the British at Detroit, and taken into British service as *Detroit*. On October 8, 1812, while escorting the Northwest Company's brig *Caledonia*, it was cut out of Fort Erie by Lieutenant Jesse Elliot and a party of US Navy sailors. (USNA)

## Lakes Erie and Huron

War on the upper lakes opened with a mixed force of British regulars, Canadian voyageurs, and local Indians attacking Fort Michilimackinac. Arriving in July 1812, they captured the fort's American garrison, which was unaware that their nation was at war. The easy victory gave the British control of the straits connecting Lakes Michigan and Huron. A month later they captured Detroit, the main bastion in the United States' Northwest Territory.

These victories gave Britain undisputed naval control of the upper lakes. British forces captured two sloops and two schooners and the United States' only armed ship, the brig *Adams*, at these American posts. *Adams* was renamed *Detroit* and added to Britain's Lake Erie Provincial Marine, consisting of the brig *General Hunter*, sloop-of-war *Queen Charlotte*, and schooner *Lady Prevost*.

The sole remaining US naval presence on Lake Erie was a small naval detachment at Buffalo, New York, commanded by Lieutenant Jesse Elliot. They

**C** **CAPTURE OF THE *GROWLER* AND *JULIA***

By August 1813, American and British forces on Lake Ontario were roughly evenly balanced. Yeo – leading the British squadron – and Chauncey – commanding the American flotilla – were cautious men, unwilling to commit to a battle without a clear advantage over the opponent. The temporary parity of August led to a series of indecisive clashes, as each commander attempted to force the other to make a mistake.

On August 10, one such battle occurred. The British, upwind of the Americans, could choose whether or not to engage. In response, Chauncey broke his squadron into two lines. He placed a line of six schooners – converted merchantmen, typically armed with one or two large guns – close to the British line. Downwind, he formed up his large warships. Chauncey was using the schooners as bait, hoping to lure Yeo's squadron into an attempt to capture the unsupported vessels.

Yeo's squadron was at this time armed primarily with short-range carronades, while Chauncey's ships were equipped with long guns, which outranged the British armament. For the British to capture the vulnerable schooners, they had to close the distance to a few hundred yards. Chauncey intended for his schooners to fall back into his battle line when Yeo swooped down to seize them.

The first part of Chauncey's plan worked – Yeo went after the schooners. When Chauncey ordered the schooners to rejoin his battle line, however, things went very wrong. Four schooners turned with the wind, and fell back as planned. The two lead schooners, *Growler* and *Julia*, tacked instead, turning into the wind. They crossed the British battle line, passing upwind of the enemy. The two small schooners had to sail back through the British line in order to rejoin the American squadron. Before they could, Yeo forced these isolated ships to surrender.

Perry commanded the gunboats at Newport Rhode Island in 1812. Seeking more active service, he asked Chauncey for a posting on the lakes. Chauncey ordered Perry to Erie to take command of American naval forces there. (USNH&HC)

were sailors without ships. On October 8, 1812, Elliot discovered *Detroit*, and a Northwest Company brig, *Caledonia*, anchored at the British Fort Erie. Elliot cut out the two ships in a boat action. While forced to burn *Detroit* to prevent its recapture, Elliot took *Caledonia* to Black Rock, New York, where it found safety under the guns of a battery.

Elliot purchased three civilian schooners at Black Rock and began converting all four into warships. Elsewhere on Lake Erie Daniel Dobbins was building two schooners for the US Navy at the new shipyard at Presque Isle.

That December Chauncey inspected Lake Erie. Concerned that Elliot's ships would not be able to reach the lake while the British controlled the north bank of the Niagara River, Chauncey ordered Elliot to halt work on the ships at Black Rock. However, Chauncey accelerated construction at Presque Isle, ordering two more gunboat-schooners to be added to the ones Dobbins had already started. He also ordered a 300-ton brig. Later, directed to increase the Lake Erie flotilla, Chauncey ordered a second brig built at Presque Isle.

To assist Dobbins, Chauncey sent shipwrights from New York, with Adam and Noah Brown to oversee construction of the additional schooners and brigs at Erie. In March 1813, Master Commandant Oliver Perry arrived at Presque Isle to take command of American naval forces on Lake Erie, and brought 100 experienced sailors with him. The shipbuilding at Presque Isle would eventually require nearly 500 men to man the vessels, and Perry's detachment provided a solid core of experienced men required for training green sailors.

Chauncey also sent Henry Eckford with workmen to Black Rock to finish arming the four ships there, resuming the work Chauncey had earlier ordered halted. *Caledonia* was armed with three large guns on pivot mounts, *Somers* was given two pivots, and *Trippe* and *Amelia*, each mounted a long 24lb gun. The American assault on Fort George drew British batteries away from the Niagara River, allowing Elliot's trapped ships at Black Rock to reach Lake Erie, and augment Perry's flotilla at Erie itself.

This buildup did not go unnoticed on the British side of the lake. Geography limited Britain's ability to reinforce its Lake Erie fleet. Three prize ships were converted into warships in early 1813. *Friend's Good Will*, a sloop captured at Michilimackinac, was given three guns and renamed *Little Belt*. A schooner, *Chippewa*, was outfitted with two howitzers, and *Erie*, a 60-ton sloop, was given two guns. Work on a new sloop-of-war began in Amherstburg that winter, but work went slowly due to limited men and supplies. When the vessel, named *Detroit*, was finally launched in July 1813, the guns intended for its battery had not arrived. Instead, Amherstburg's fortifications were stripped of guns to arm *Detroit*.

The biggest challenge the British faced was finding men to man these ships. *Queen Charlotte* – with 20 guns – had a crew of only 75 men in early 1813, and *Lady Prevost* had only 43 – half its intended complement. Perry, while he frequently complained about the quality of his seamen, received regular reinforcements of sailors from the Atlantic coast, and successfully recruited more from lakes mariners. Of the 540 men manning his flotilla at the Battle of Lake Erie, three-quarters were experienced sailors. By contrast, Britain's Lake Erie squadron was sporadically reinforced. Robert Barclay, Perry's opposite number, only arrived in June, and he brought a handful of officers and two dozen Royal Navy sailors.

Barclay made a creditable defense of Lake Erie. Perry's fleet outnumbered Barclay in both men and weight of metal, but in July the just-finished brigs *Niagara* and *Lawrence* were trapped behind a sandbar in Presque Isle Bay. To cross the bar they had to be stripped of guns and refitted in the open roadstead. Barclay blockaded Erie in July, penning *Lawrence* and *Niagara* inside. As long as Barclay was there Perry could not get his brigs into the lake without risking their capture.

Barclay could not remain in position indefinitely, however, and in mid June he lifted the blockade to resupply. He was gone only four days, but when Barclay returned, he found the American ships – including both brigs – anchored in line-of-battle off Erie – Perry dragged the two ships across the bar in Barclay's absence. The brigs' guns had not yet been reinstalled, but Perry bluffed Barclay into believing they were armed. Barclay withdrew to Amherstburg to await completion of *Detroit*.

Even with *Detroit*, Barclay's squadron was outclassed. Perry's force had nearly half again the number of guns, and twice the weight of metal. By the time *Detroit* was ready, Barclay had only 60 Royal Navy officers and men, and 110 men who had previously served with the Provincial Marine. He was forced to fill out his crews with 230 soldiers from the army in Upper Canada. To conserve manpower he laid up *Erie*.

Despite the American advantages, when the two fleets finally met off Put-in-Bay a surprisingly close battle ensued. This situation was due to piecemeal commitment of the American forces into the battle. Fought under light winds, the American van – schooners *Ariel* and *Scorpion* and the brig *Lawrence* – became separated from the rest of Perry's ships. Elliot, commanding *Niagara*, refused to join the battle. He later claimed that he did not want to break the line of battle to pass the sluggish *Caledonia*, immediately behind *Lawrence*.

*Lawrence*, fighting the entire British force virtually single-handedly, was reduced to a wreck. In turn, the brig hammered the main British ships. Unable to continue the fight on *Lawrence*, Perry transferred to *Niagara* in an open boat. *Lawrence* surrendered shortly afterwards. Once aboard *Niagara*, Perry took it into the battle. Barclay's flotilla, badly battered from fighting *Lawrence*, now yielded. Perry captured the entire British force – two ships, two brigs, one schooner, and one sloop. Command of Lake Erie passed to the United States.

While the United States dominated Lake Erie for the rest of the war, the British staged a comeback on the upper lakes in 1814. Four US schooners – *Little Belt*, *Chippewa* (prizes taken at Lake Erie), *Ariel*, and *Trippe* – were sent to Buffalo by Elliot, but were trapped there by winter. When an overland British raid struck Buffalo in December 1813, all four vessels were burned. In 1814, Captain Arthur Sinclair – who replaced Perry – took the Lake Erie fleet into Lake Huron to recapture Michilimackinac. The joint army-navy force had to drag *Niagara* and *Lawrence* over shallows in the St Clair River to get them into Lake Huron.

The invasion force was rebuffed at Mackinac Island, losing schooners *Scorpion* and *Tigress* in Georgian Bay to a British cutting-out expedition. Having almost lost the remaining ships in a storm, the force returned to Detroit. The schooners were added to the Royal Navy as *Confiance* and *Surprise*. When Sinclair returned to Lake Erie, he discovered two schooners – *Somers* and *Ohio* – had also been lost to cutting-out operations off Fort Erie. They became *Huron* and *Sauk*.

Robert Barclay briefly commanded Royal Navy forces on Lake Ontario before being sent to take charge at Lake Erie. (USNH&HC)

The action that transformed the Battle of Lake Erie from a potential British victory to an American triumph was Perry's decision to abandon the unworkable *Lawrence* and transfer to the *Niagara* by small boat. Bringing the previously undamaged *Niagara* into action forced the immobile and exhausted British to surrender. (LOC)

## Lake Champlain

Neither the United States nor Great Britain had armed ships on Lake Champlain when the War of 1812 began. The last British warship on Lake Champlain, sloop *Royal Edward*, was launched in 1794 and had decayed into senility. The Americans built two 40ft gunboats in 1809, but by 1812 both were beached at a small naval station at Vergennes, Vermont. Although Lake Champlain was a major trade highway between the United States and Lower Canada prior to the war, neither nation intended it as an invasion route in 1812.

Lieutenant Sydney Smith – the US Navy officer in charge at Vergennes – refitted the gunboats and armed one, stationing both at Plattsburg, New York, at the lake's northern end. The US Army purchased six commercial sloops on the lake, and was building bateaux – small flat-bottomed boats – to carry troops. The sloops were soon assigned to the navy. To command them, Lieutenant Thomas MacDonough was sent from Portsmouth, Maine, where he then commanded a gunboat flotilla. He arrived in October 1812, with 25 officers and men from his former command.

After a brief tussle with Major General Henry Dearborn, commanding US Army forces around Lake Champlain, over control of the sloops, MacDonough outfitted three as warships. By November, MacDonough commanded a flotilla consisting of *President* (8 guns), *Growler* (7 guns), and *Eagle* (7 guns), and the two pre-war gunboats, each of which were armed with a single long 12lb gun. Over the winter, MacDonough improved the sloops, adding a quarterdeck and four guns to each.

The British reacted to these American preparations by refortifying Isle aux Noix and sending three two-gun galleys there from Quebec. Then that summer the British unexpectedly augmented their fleet.

**D** ## LOSS OF THE *SCOURGE*

Lakes schooners were extremely sensitive to shifts in the hull's center-of-gravity. Placing artillery on their decks made these otherwise stable ships highly unstable. Unexpected wind shifts could easily capsize armed schooners – as happened on August 7, 1813. The American armed schooners *Hamilton* and *Scourge* were anchored off Twelve Mile Creek following an inconclusive battle with the British Squadron on Lake Ontario near the Niagara River. Suddenly, in the middle of the night, a lakes storm blew up. Caught unprepared, both ships were rolled on their beam ends and sank. Of the 96 men aboard both ships, only six survived. Ned Myers, an ordinary seaman aboard Scourge left a dramatic account of the sinking in his memoirs. In part it read:

*I now remember to have heard a strange rushing noise to windward ... though it made no impression on me at the time ... there not being a breath of air, and no motion to the water ... [Suddenly] a flash of lightning almost blinded me. The thunder came at the next instant, and with it a rushing of winds that fairly smothered the clap.*

*The instant I was aware there was a squall, I sprang for the jib-sheet ... I jumped on a man named Leonard Lewis, and called on him to lend me a hand. I next let fly the larboard, or lee top-sail-sheet, got hold of the clew-line, and, assisted by Lewis, got the clew half up ... The water was now up to my breast, and I knew the schooner must go over.*

*... the schooner was filled with the shrieks and cries of the men to leeward, who were lying jammed under the guns, shot-boxes, shot, and other heavy things that had gone down as the vessel fell over.*

Thomas MacDonough commanded a gunboat flotilla at Portland when he was tapped to command US Navy forces on Lake Champlain. During the Barbary Wars MacDonough, then a midshipman, participated in the 1804 burning of the frigate Philadelphia in Tripoli harbor. (USNH&HC)

Lake Champlain remained a commercial highway throughout the War of 1812, used by New York and Vermont farmers and lumbermen selling food and timber in Canada. While this activity constituted trading with the enemy, the War of 1812 was unpopular in New England, and the British paid *in specie*. To end this smuggling, MacDonough sent Smith with *Eagle* and *Growler* to patrol the northern end of the lake in June 1813. The over-aggressive Smith took his ships up the Richelieu River, crossing the border into Quebec.

On June 3, two miles from Isle aux Noix, in a stretch of river too narrow to turn around easily, Smith's ships were ambushed by British artillery and marksmen hidden on the river's banks. *Eagle* was captured after grounding. *Growler* surrendered. Both were added to the Royal Navy – *Eagle* as *Shannon*, and *Growler* as *Broke*. The British now outnumbered and outgunned the United States on Lake Champlain.

To compound American discomfiture, in July Yeo sent Commander Daniel Pring with six naval officers to take charge. When Pring arrived, he found Captain Thomas Everard, who commanded HMS *Wasp*, already there with 80 men. Everard temporarily left his ship at Prevost's request, and joined forces with Pring and Lieutenant Colonel John Murray to raid Lake Champlain. On July 29, the expedition left Isle aux Noix, with Royal Navy ships escorting 1,000 soldiers in bateaux. "Murray's Raid" attacked Plattsburg on July 31, burning public buildings, and seizing military and naval stores, crossed the lake to Swanson, Vermont, burning an American army base, and then sailed to Burlington, Vermont.

They found MacDonough's fleet there. MacDonough could not meet the British on open water, but anchored his ships – *President* and the two gunboats – in line of battle. Everard decided he could not lure MacDonough out, so he returned to Isle aux Noix capturing several merchant ships along the way. Everard then returned to *Wasp*, leaving Pring in charge at Lake Champlain.

Both sides then began adding ships. MacDonough had bought two new sloops – *Preble* and *Montgomery*, and armed them with nine guns each. He also armed three other small sloops with two or three guns each, to beef up his squadron temporarily.

Pring created a shipyard at Isle aux Noix and started work on a 370-ton 16-gun brig (initially named *Niagara*, but renamed *Linnet*) and five gunboats. All were ready by spring 1814. Having temporarily defeated Napoleon, Britain was transferring Wellington's veterans to North America – and Lake Champlain offered the best route to move this army from Canada into the United States.

By November, MacDonough had learned about the British shipbuilding, and he sought permission to expand his force. The Navy Department approved MacDonough's plans to build gunboats, then, in February 1814, he sent Noah Brown to Vergennes to build larger ships. Over the next three months, Brown built six row galley gunboats and a 26-gun sloop-of-war, and converted an unfinished steamboat into a 19-gun schooner-rigged warship.

When the British made their first foray of 1814 into Lake Champlain in May, they discovered that the American squadron was stronger than their own. Pring was forced to withdraw. Seeking more firepower, Pring visited Quebec to investigate whether he could use the two disassembled brigs sent from Britain. Their draft was too deep for Lake Champlain, so he chose to build a new ship – a frigate – at Isle aux Noix. When MacDonough heard about this development he had Brown build one more warship – a brig, that MacDonough named *Eagle*.

The two sides finally met on September 11, off Plattsburg Bay on the north side of Lake Champlain. In addition to *Broke* and *Shannon* – renamed *Finch* and *Chub* – the British had the brig *Linnet*, 11 rowed gunboats, and their still-incomplete 37-gun frigate, *Confiance*. Pring was not in charge. Superseded as squadron commander by Captain George Downie, Pring instead commanded *Linnet*. The British squadron was accompanied by an 11,000-man army led by Prevost. Opposing Downie's ships was MacDonough's squadron – the 26-gun sloop-of-war *Saratoga*, 17-gun schooner *Ticonderoga*, brig *Eagle*, sloop *Preble*, Brown's six galleys, and four gunboats.

MacDonough's initial squadron on Lake Champlain was made up of converted sloops. His two most powerful vessels, *Growler* (shown) and *Eagle*, were captured on June 2, 1813, when they were ambushed by shore-based artillery while pursuing British gunboats. (Courtesy of Kevin Crisman)

MacDonough anchored his fleet in a line between Cumberland Head and Crab Island. The British reached Plattsburg on September 10, but were unable to attack due to adverse winds. The next day, when the wind shifted, they sailed up to the American line, anchored, and opened fire. The battle was decided by the five purpose-built warships. *Chub*, *Finch*, and *Preble* were soon forced out of the battle. *Ticonderoga* fought the British gunboats, while *Eagle* and *Saratoga* battled *Linnet* and *Confiance*.

Inexperience showed on both sides. Overloading dismounted most of *Saratoga*'s guns on its engaged side. The British crews, after a few deadly accurate broadsides, worked their guns' elevation quoins loose, and began firing over the *Saratoga*. Victory was a matter of superior American preparation, as MacDonough had anchored his ships so that they could be pivoted, and could bring untouched broadsides to bear on the British. When the battle ended, all the British ships were American prizes.

The British Army – which was supposed to attack when the first naval guns fired – instead sat passively until the naval action ended. Then they withdrew back to Canada, ending the threat of invasion for 1814 and effectively ending the War of 1812 on Lake Champlain.

## Afterwards

The navies on the inland lakes vanished as quickly as they appeared. The Treaty of Ghent ended the War of 1812. Ratified by the United States Senate in February 1815, it suspended hostilities in February. The lakes warships were still laid up for the winter. Work continued on ships under construction during the winter of 1814 and 1815, especially on Lake Ontario, where both sides were building ships-of-the-line, but construction was suspended once word of the peace reached the lakes. Few ships were pulled out of winter storage in 1815, by both nations.

HMS *Linnet*, a 16-gun brig, was built at Isle aux Noix, in late 1813. The sail plan is a reconstruction based on examination of *Linnet's* hull following a 1995 excavation. (Courtesy of Erika Lea Washburn)

On Lake Ontario, the United States commissioned three ships: brigs *Oneida* and *Jones* and the schooner *Sylph*. Left in ordinary, anchored at Sackett's Harbor were the sloops-of-war and frigates built with such urgency during the previous two years. On Lake Champlain the entire American flotilla was left laid up. On Lake Erie, *Lawrence* and prizes *Queen Charlotte* and *Detroit* were sunk at Misery Bay, near Erie, Pennsylvania for preservation. *Niagara* was kept in commission, but only as a receiving ship – a floating barracks.

The United States quickly sold most converted merchantmen and some smaller warships. The converted schooners on Lake Ontario were auctioned off in May. The smaller warships and schooners on Lake Erie were also put up for sale in May, with the last one, *Lady Prevost*, sold by autumn. The sloops and four gunboats on Lake Champlain were gone by July.

The Battle of Lake Champlain (or Plattsburg) as seen from shore. The ships are, left to right: *Linnet* (far left), *Eagle*, *Chub* (almost invisible between *Eagle* and *Saratoga*), *Saratoga*, *Confiance*, *Ticonderoga*, and *Preble*. On the right (top to bottom) are *Montgomery*, *Finch* (aground), and *President*. *Montgomery* and *President* were transports in 1814. (LOC)

Great Britain, less penurious than the American government, kept more ships in commission. On Lake Ontario, *Prince Regent*, *Niagara*, *Montreal*, *Star*, and *Netley* were kept in commission, albeit with reduced crews, with *Montreal* converted into a transport. The rest, including the frigate *Psyche* launched in December 1814, were laid up. By contrast, the British fleet on Lake Champlain consisted only of gunboats. These were laid up at Isle aux Noix. On the upper lakes four schooners were kept in commission in Georgian Bay.

Ambitious building programs were abandoned, and only a handful of intended ships were built. The United States built *Ghent*, a 50-ton schooner, on Lake Erie in 1815, while the British built a small transport on Lake Ontario. On the upper lakes, British plans to create four big frigates were shelved. Instead two ships, an armed schooner named *Tecumseth* and transport *Bee*, were built by the British in Georgian Bay.

The Rush–Bagot Treaty, negotiated in 1816, demilitarized the lakes. It limited each nation to one armed warship each on Lake Champlain and Lake Ontario, and two each on the upper lakes, none in excess of 100 tons. Both sides kept ships in storage for the next few years, but by 1825 the United

**E**    **THE BATTLE OF LAKE CHAMPLAIN/PLATTSBURG**

The climax of the Battle of Lake Champlain occurred at 1040hrs on September 11, 1814, nearly an hour after the start of the battle. British sloops – *Finch* and *Chub* – were out of the battle. The American schooner, *Ticonderoga* was occupied with fighting British gunboats.

Victory was to be decided through a slugging match between the four largest ships in the battle. The British brig *Linnet* and frigate *Confiance* were paired against the American brig *Eagle* and sloop-of-war *Saratoga*. Both sides were heavily damaged in the first hour of the battle, with the Americans taking the worst of the exchange. *Eagle*, hard pressed by *Linnet* and *Confiance*, cut its cable at 1030hrs, and drifted past *Saratoga*. There, sheltered from *Linnet's* gunfire by *Saratoga*, it anchored by the stern, so its port broadside could be brought to bear. From that position, however, *Eagle* could only fire on *Confiance*, and only at long distance.

By then, *Saratoga* had lost every gun on its engaged, starboard side. British gunfire dismounted some of the guns, and its inexperienced crew had overset the rest by overloading the guns. The two British ships were also hard hit, but they still had guns that could fire on the now-helpless *Saratoga*.

But Thomas MacDonough had anchored *Saratoga* on "springs" – a second, slack cable was attached to the anchor, and passed through the stern gunports. Pulling this cable in pulled *Saratoga's* stern towards the anchor. MacDonough sent every available hand to *Saratoga's* capstan at 1040hrs, pivoting *Saratoga* through 170 degrees. This maneuver turned its undamaged port battery to where it could fire on the British ships. At 1100hrs, ten minutes after *Saratoga* resumed firing, *Confiance* – which only had four guns that could fire – struck. The now-outgunned *Linnet* followed suit 15 minutes later.

States closed their naval stations at Sackett's Harbor, Presque Isle, and Whitehall (on Lake Champlain). The British followed suit a few years later, closing their lakes station in 1834. The warship age on the lakes was over.

## THE SHIPS

Note on statistics: LBP is length between parallels – typically the distance between the stem and sternpost. This is the best approximation of the waterline length. LD is the length of the upper or gun deck. Breadth is maximum breadth or width of the ship. Depth of Hold measures the depth of the hold between the bottom of the ship and the berth deck. Draft is the maximum loaded waterline. Displacement is given in long tons. Dates are as accurate as possible.

Values were extracted from numerous sources, including *The Dictionary of American Naval Fighting Ships*, Chapelle's *The History of the American Sailing Navy*, Malcomson's *Warships of the Great Lakes*, Winfield's *British Warships in the Age of Sail*, Caney's *Sailing Warships of the United States Navy*, and a collection of research papers on Lakes Warships written by Kevin Crisman and his graduate students. Malcomson's book was the primary source, unless modified by additional information.

Units are in imperial measure – feet, inches, tons, and pounds – reflecting contemporary practice. Where limited information was unavailable, the author calculated values from what was available. The lack of uniformity in the shipbuilding industry – especially on the lakes frontiers – and the confusion inherent in the haste that many of these ships were built – means that some values given are best-guess approximations. Armament listed for the ships is sometimes speculative, especially for those ships that were never commissioned.

The ships are arranged here by the lake on which they were built – Lake Ontario, Lake Erie (and the upper lakes that could be reached from Lake Erie: St Clair and Huron), and Lake Champlain (and the Richelieu River). Ships were often captured (and sometimes recaptured) during the War of 1812, but they are also

**ABOVE**

USS *Superior*, in ordinary after the War of 1812. A large ocean-going 44-gun frigate built for the United States during the War of 1812, it gave Chauncey's squadron temporary control of Lake Ontario. (AC)

**ABOVE RIGHT**

Sackett's Harbor was the main base for the US Navy on Lake Ontario. By 1814 it was a major shipbuilding center, but the New York river network meant supplies either had to travel overland, or be shipped along the Lake Ontario coast from Oswego. (AC)

The British flotilla on Lake Ontario in 1814, seen anchored off Oswego. From left to right the ships are: *Star* (originally *Lord Melville*), *Charwell* (ex-*Earl of Moira*), *Niagara* (ex-*Royal George*), *Montreal* (ex-*Wolfe*), *Magnet* (ex-*Sir Sidney Smith*), *Princess Royal*, and *Prince Regent*. The painting was made by Captain William Steele, Royal Marines, a participant. (LOC)

arranged by nationality of origin – British then American. Vessels constructed as warships are listed separately from merchant craft that were already on the lakes, then purchased and converted to warships. Small, rowed vessels are omitted. Every category lists ships by launch date, regardless of when they entered naval service.

# Lake Ontario
## Warships constructed by Great Britain

### *Earl of Moira* (ship-rigged sloop-of-war)

| | |
|---|---|
| Dimensions | LD: 70ft 6in / Breadth: 23ft 8in / Depth of Hold: 7ft / Draft: 8ft 6in |
| Displacement | 168.6 tons |
| Complement | 127 |
| Armament | 1812: 10 x 18lb carronades<br>1813: 14 x 24lb carronades, 2 x 9lb long guns<br>1814:12 x 24lb carronades, 1 x 18lb long gun (pivot) |
| Built | 1805, Kingston, Upper Canada |
| Entered Service | 1805, Provincial Marine |

Originally intended as a brig or snow, it was subsequently rigged with three masts. It was re-rigged as a brig during a late 1813 refit. Renamed *Charwell* in 1814, it became a powder hulk in 1816, then a receiving ship in 1827. Sold in 1837.

### *Duke of Gloucester* (armed schooner)

| | |
|---|---|
| Dimensions | LBP: 60ft / Breadth: 18ft |
| Displacement | 65 tons |
| Armament | 12 x 6lb long guns |
| Built | 1807, Kingston, Upper Canada |
| Entered Service | 1807, Provincial Marine |

The ship was at York undergoing a rebuild when Chauncey's squadron captured York in April 1813, and it was taken to Sackett's Harbor as a prize and renamed *York*.

### *Royal George* (ship-rigged sloop-of-war)

| | |
|---|---|
| Dimensions | LD: 96ft 9in / Breadth: 27ft 7in / Depth of Hold: 11ft / Draft: 13ft 11in |
| Displacement | 330.2 tons |
| Complement | 204 |
| Armament | 1812: 20 x 32lb carronades<br>1813: 2 x 68lb carronades, 16 x 32lb carronades, 2 x 18lb long guns<br>1814: 18 x 32lb carronades, 1 x 24lb long gun (pivot), 2 x 18lb long guns |
| Built | 1809, Kingston, Upper Canada |
| Entered Service | 1809, Provincial Marine |

Built by master shipwright William Bell, *Royal George* was the largest warship on the lakes when launched. Renamed *Niagara* in 1814, it was condemned as unfit in 1816, rebuilt in 1820, and sold into merchant service in 1837.

### *Prince Regent* (armed schooner)

| | |
|---|---|
| Dimensions | LD: 72ft 6in / Breadth: 21ft 2in / Depth of Hold: 7ft 3in / Draft: 9ft 4in |
| Displacement | 142.7 tons |
| Complement | 150 |
| Armament | 1812: 10 x 12lb carronades, 2 x 6lb long guns<br>1813: 10 x 18lb carronades, 2 x 9lb long guns<br>1814: 10 x 18lb carronades, 1 x 24lb long gun (pivot) |
| Built | 1812, York, Upper Canada |
| Entered Service | 1812, Provincial Marine |

Designed and built by John Dennis. Renamed *Lord Beresford* in 1813. Re-rigged as a brig in 1814 and renamed *Netley*. In commission through 1816 with a reduced crew, it was laid up soon afterwards, and sold in the 1830s.

### Sir George Prevost (ship-rigged sloop-of-war)

| | |
|---|---|
| Dimensions | LD: 101ft 9in / Breadth: 30ft 6in / Depth of Hold: 11ft / Draft: 12ft 4in |
| Displacement | 426.2 tons |
| Complement | 224 |
| Armament | 1813: 2 x 68lb carronades, 18 x 18lb carronades, 2 x 12lb long guns<br>1814: 4 x 68lb carronades, 8 x 32lb carronades, 1 x 24lb long gun (pivot),<br>8 x 18lb long guns |
| Built | 1813, Kingston, Upper Canada |
| Entered Service | 1813, Royal Navy |

A larger version of *Royal George*, *Sir George Prevost* was renamed *Wolfe* immediately after launch. Renamed *Montreal* in 1814. Re-armed as a transport after the war's end, remaining in service until laid up in 1817, and sold in 1832. A sister ship, *Sir Isaac Brock*, was burned while under construction in York in 1813, to prevent its capture.

### Lord Melville (brig-rigged sloop-of-war)

| | |
|---|---|
| Dimensions | LD: 71ft 7in / Breadth: 24ft 8in / Depth of Hold: 8ft / Draft: 9ft 9in |
| Displacement | 186.5 tons |
| Complement | 98 |
| Armament | 1813–14: 12 x 32lb carronades, 2 x 18lb long guns |
| Built | 1813, Kingston, Upper Canada |
| Entered Service | 1813, Royal Navy |

Served in Yeo's squadron in 1813. Renamed *Star* in 1814. Converted to a transport in 1815. Paid off in 1816, and sold in 1837.

### Prince Regent (frigate)

(see plate F)

### Princess Charlotte (frigate)

| | |
|---|---|
| Dimensions | LBP: 121ft / Breadth: 37ft 8in / Depth of Hold: 8ft 8in / Draft: 17ft |
| Displacement | 756 tons |
| Complement | 280 |
| Armament | 2 x 68lb carronades, 16 x 32lb carronades, 24 x 24lb long guns |
| Built | 1814, Kingston, Upper Canada |
| Entered Service | 1814, Royal Navy |

Originally intended as a transport brig named *Vittoria*, *Princess Charlotte* was modified into a larger ship on the stocks by George Record. Manpower and material shortages delayed completion until the spring of 1814. Renamed *Burlington* in September 1814, it remained in commission through 1816 when it was laid up. Ordered sold in 1833, but no buyers appeared. Afterwards sank in Deadman Bay.

### St Lawrence (ship-of-the-line)

| | |
|---|---|
| Dimensions | LBP: 191ft 2in / Breadth: 52ft 6in / Depth of Hold: 18ft 6in / Draft: 20ft |
| Displacement | 2,305 tons |
| Complement | 700 |
| Armament | 1813: 2 x 68lb carronades, 34 x 32lb carronades, 34 x 24lb long guns, 34 x 32lb long guns |
| Built | 1814, Kingston, Upper Canada |
| Entered Service | 1814, Royal Navy |

The first and only lakes ship-of-the-line launched and commissioned, *St Lawrence* served as Yeo's flagship from October to December 1814. Laid up in 1815, and sold at auction in 1832. The hull served as a storage pier for Morton's Brewery in Kingston.

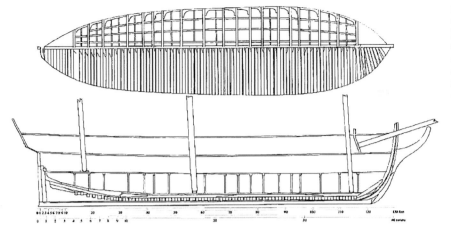

HMS *Princess Charlotte* was one of three Royal Navy frigates built on Lake Ontario. This drawing of its lines is a reconstruction based on archeological examination of its wreck in Deadman Bay. (Courtesy of Daniel Walker)

### *Psyche* (frigate)

| | |
|---|---|
| Dimensions | LBP: 130ft / Breadth: 36ft 7in / Depth of Hold: 10ft 3in / Draft: 9ft 8in |
| Displacement | 769 tons |
| Complement | 280 |
| Armament | 28 x 32lb carronades, 28 x 24lb long guns |
| Built | 1814, Kingston, Upper Canada |
| Entered Service | 1815, Royal Navy |

The only ship to emerge from a project to build prefabricated warships in Canada. Sufficient prefabricated frames at Montreal were shipped to Kingston to build the *Psyche*. Launched in December 1814, the frigate was laid up in 1815. Ordered sold in 1833, no buyer was found. It sank at its moorings in the late 1830s.

### *Wolfe, Canada* (ships-of-the-line)

| | |
|---|---|
| Dimensions | LBP: 191ft 3in / Breadth: 50ft 8in / Depth of Hold: 18ft 6in / Draft: 20ft |
| Displacement | 2,152.4 tons |
| Complement | 700 |
| Armament | 1813: 36 x 32lb carronades, 76 x 24lb long guns |
| Built | Work started 1814, Kingston, Upper Canada |
| Entered Service | Never |

Construction started in 1814, but was suspended in 1815 at the war's end. The hulls were broken up on the stocks in 1832.

## Schooners Purchased by Great Britain

### *Sir Sydney Smith* (armed schooner)

| | |
|---|---|
| Displacement | 187 tons |
| Complement | 70 |
| Armament | 1812–13: 10 x 32lb carronades, 2 x 12lb long guns<br>1814: 10 x 24lb carronades, 1 x 9lb long gun (pivot) |
| Built | 1808, Mississauga Point, Upper Canada |
| Entered Service | 1812, Provincial Marine |

Built for Upper Canada's civil government as *Governor Simcoe*, but purchased for the Provincial Marine in 1812, and renamed *Sir Sydney Smith*. Re-rigged as a brig in 1814 and renamed *Magnet*. Trapped by Chauncey's squadron while carrying munitions on August 5, 1814, it was run aground and burnt to avoid capture.

# Warships constructed by the United States

### *Oneida* (brig-of-war)

(see plate G)

### *Madison* (ship-rigged sloop-of-war)

| | |
|---|---|
| Dimensions | LBP: 112ft / Breadth: 32ft 6in / Draft: 11ft 6in |
| Displacement | 580 tons |
| Complement | 200 |
| Armament | 1812–13: 20 x 32lb carronades, 4 x 18lb long guns<br>1814: 8 x 32lb carronades, 15 x 18lb long guns (1 mounted as pivot) |
| Built | 1812, Sackett's Harbor, New York |
| Entered Service | 1813, US Navy |

Designed and built by Henry Eckford, *Madison* was the first American sloop-of-war on the lakes. Laid up in 1815, and sold into merchant service as *General Brady* in 1825, sailing on Lake Ontario for a few seasons.

### *Lady of the Lake* (armed schooner)

| | |
|---|---|
| Dimensions | LBP: 65ft |
| Displacement | 89 tons |
| Complement | 40 |
| Armament | 1 x 9lb long gun (pivot) |
| Built | 1813, Sackett's Harbor, New York |
| Entered Service | 1813, US Navy |

Built by Henry Eckford as a dispatch boat, *Lady of the Lake* captured *Lady Murray* – an English schooner – in a two-ship action on June 16, 1813. Remained in commission until 1817, the only American warship on Lake Ontario. Laid up in 1818, sold to merchant service in 1825, and lost off Oswego in December, 1826.

### *Sylph* (armed schooner)

| | |
|---|---|
| Dimensions | LBP: 65ft |
| Displacement | 300 tons |
| Complement | 70 |
| Armament | 1813: 4 x 32lb long guns (pivots), 6 x 6lb long guns<br>1814: 16 x 24lb carronades, 2 x 9lb long guns |
| Built | 1813, Sackett's Harbor, New York |
| Entered Service | 1813, US Navy |

Designed and built by Henry Eckford. Laid up at Sackett's Harbor in 1815, it sank at its moorings in 1823. Sold and broken up in 1825.

**BELOW**

*Lady of the Lake* was a dispatch schooner built for the US Navy on Lake Ontario by Henry Eckford. On June 18, 1813, while patrolling the Canadian shore, it fell in with British transport *Lady Murray*, and captured it. (USNA)

**BELOW RIGHT**

No plans exist for the brigs *Jefferson* and *Jones*. The hull design was based on the 1813 *Peacock*-class sloops-of-war, one of which is shown here. (AC)

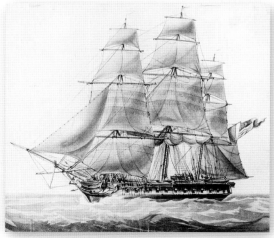

### General Pike (ship-rigged sloop-of-war)

| | |
|---|---|
| Dimensions | LBP: 145ft / Breadth: 38ft 6in / Draft: 11ft 6in |
| Displacement | 875 tons |
| Complement | 300 |
| Armament | 26 x 24lb long guns (2 mounted as pivots) |
| Built | 1812, Sackett's Harbor, New York |
| Entered Service | 1813, US Navy |

*General Pike* was designed and built by Henry Eckford. Its unfinished hull was accidentally set on fire when the British raided Sackett's Harbor on May 29, 1813. The fires were doused before they caused major damage, and the ship entered service in July. Laid up at Sackett's Harbor in 1815. Sold and broken up in 1825.

### Jefferson, Jones (brigs-of-war)

| | |
|---|---|
| Dimensions | LBP: 122ft 11in / Breadth: 33ft 2in / Draft: 12ft 9in |
| Displacement | 500 tons |
| Complement | 160 |
| Armament | 16 x 42lb carronades, 4 x 24lb long guns |
| Built | 1814, Sackett's Harbor, New York |
| Entered Service | 1814, US Navy |

Based on the *Peacock*-class sloops-of-war, these two brigs were built by Henry Eckford. Laid up in late 1814, *Jefferson* remained in ordinary at Sackett's Harbor until sold in April 1825. *Jones* served as a receiving ship from 1815 through 1820 and was sold in 1825.

### Superior (frigate)

| | |
|---|---|
| Dimensions | LBP: 180ft / Breadth: 43ft / Draft: 17ft |
| Displacement | 1,580 tons |
| Complement | 500 |
| Armament | 26 x 42lb carronades, 30 x 32lb long guns, 2 x 24lb long guns |
| Built | 1814, Sackett's Harbor, New York |
| Entered Service | 1814, US Navy |

Built by Henry Eckford, *Superior* was comparable in size to the ocean-going *Guerriere*-class frigates built in 1814. Launched May 1, 1814, 89 days after its keel was laid. Laid up in 1815 at Sackett's Harbor. Sold and broken up in 1825.

### Mohawk (frigate)

| | |
|---|---|
| Dimensions | LBP: 155ft / Breadth: 37ft 6in / Draft: 15ft 6in |
| Displacement | 1,350 tons |
| Complement | 350 |
| Armament | 16 x 32lb carronades, 26 x 24lb long guns |
| Built | 1814, Sackett's Harbor, New York |
| Entered Service | 1814, US Navy |

Construction of *Mohawk* began a week after *Superior*'s launching. Built by Henry Eckford, *Mohawk* was launched just 34 days after building started. Laid up in 1815 at Sackett's Harbor. Reported unfit for repair in 1821, and broken up.

### New Orleans, Chippewa (ships-of-the-line)

| | |
|---|---|
| Dimensions | LBP: 204ft / Breadth: 56ft |
| Displacement | 2,805 tons |
| Complement | 350 |
| Armament | 24 x 32lb carronades, 63 x 32lb long guns |
| Built | 1814–15, Sackett's Harbor, New York |
| Entered Service | Never |

Designed and built by Noah and Adam Brown, both were laid down in October 1814, for completion by the following spring. Construction suspended at war's end, and both remained on the stocks. *Chippewa* sold and broken up in 1833. *New Orleans* retained until 1883 before being scrapped.

## Schooners purchased by the United States

### Fair American

| | |
|---|---|
| Displacement | 82 tons |
| Complement | 52 |
| Armament | 1 x 32lb long gun, 1 x 24lb long gun (both pivots) |
| Launched | 1804, Oswego, New York; purchased 1812 |

*Fair American* served as a warship in 1812–13 and a transport in 1814. Sold in 1815.

### Asp (sloop)

| | |
|---|---|
| Displacement | 57 tons |
| Complement | 45 |
| Armament | 1 x 32lb long gun (pivot), 2 x 6lb long guns |
| Launched | 1808, Mississauga, Upper Canada; purchased 1813 |

As British merchant vessel *Elizabeth*, captured by *Growler* in 1812. Condemned and purchased into the US Navy in 1813. Served as both a warship and transport during the war. Sold 1815.

### Growler

| | |
|---|---|
| Displacement | 81 tons |
| Complement | 35 |
| Armament | 1 x 24lb long gun (pivot), 4 x 4lb long guns |
| Launched | 1809, Ogdensburg, New York; purchased 1812 |

Formerly the civilian *Experiment*. Captured by the British on August 10, 1813, it was recaptured by the Americans on October 5, 1813, and returned to service as a warship. Again retaken by the British at Oswego on May 5, 1814, it subsequently became the British warship *Hamilton*. Sold in 1815.

### Pert

| | |
|---|---|
| Displacement | 50 tons |
| Complement | 35 |
| Armament | 1 x 32lb long gun (pivot), 2 x 4lb long guns |
| Launched | 1809, Ogdensburg, New York; purchased 1812 |

Civilian *Collector*. Sold May 1815.

## PRINCE REGENT (FRIGATE)

Dimensions: LBP: 155ft 10in / Breadth: 43ft 1in / Depth of Hold: 9ft 2in / Draft: 16ft 4in
Displacement: 1,293.5 tons
Complement: 280
Armament: 1814: 4 x 68lb carronades, 24 x 32lb carronades, 28 x 24lb long guns
Built: 1814, Kingston, Upper Canada
Entered Service: 1814, Royal Navy

Built in response to the new American sloops-of-war on Lake Ontario, *Prince Regent* was designed by John Goudie, a master shipbuilder from Quebec. He designed a large, spar-decked frigate, with two full banks of guns. Construction started in August 1813, overseen by Patrick Fleming, but shortages of both building materials and shipyard workers delayed its completion until 1814. It was finally launched on April 14, 1814, and was in commission by the beginning of May. *Prince Regent*, the first frigate built on Lake Ontario, or any other inland lakes for that matter, allowed the British to dominate Lake Ontario until the midsummer appearance of the American frigates.

The vessel was renamed *Kingston* in December 1814, but saw no active service in 1815. After the war's end, it remained in service with a reduced crew. Finally laid up in 1817 following the negotiation of the Rush–Bagot Treaty, which demilitarized the Great Lakes and Lake Champlain, it remained in ordinary through the 1830s. The vessel was ordered to be sold in 1832, yet no buyer could be found, so it remained anchored in Deadman Bay near Kingston, Upper Canada. It sank at its moorings sometime after 1832.

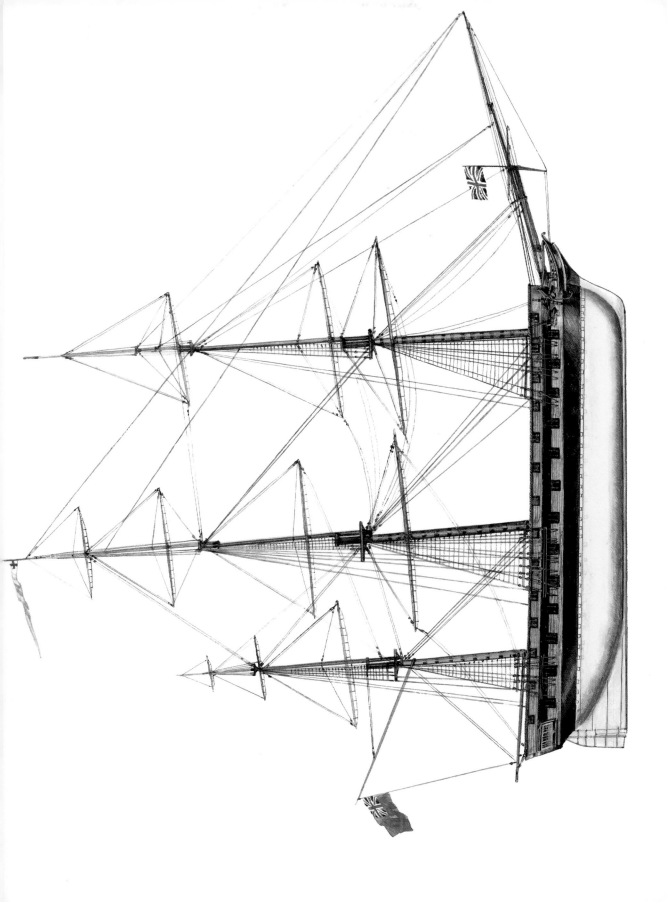

### Hamilton

| | |
|---|---|
| Displacement | 112 tons |
| Complement | 53 |
| Armament | 8 x 18lb carronades, 1 x 12lb long gun (pivot) |
| Launched | 1809, Ogdensburg, New York; purchased 1812 |

Civilian *Diana*. Sank in a squall off Twelve Mile Creek, Upper Canada.

### Ontario

| | |
|---|---|
| Displacement | 53 tons |
| Complement | 35 |
| Armament | 1 x 32lb long gun, 1 x 12lb long gun (both pivots) |
| Launched | 1809, Lewiston, New York; purchased 1812 |

Sold back to merchant service in 1815.

### Conquest

| | |
|---|---|
| Displacement | 82 tons |
| Complement | 40 |
| Armament | 2 x 24lb long guns (both pivots), 1 x 6lb long gun |
| Launched | 1810, Ogdensburg, New York; purchased 1812 |

Civilian *Genesee Packet*. Sold 1815.

### Governor Tompkins

| | |
|---|---|
| Displacement | 96 tons |
| Complement | 64 |
| Armament | 2 x 18lb carronades, 1 x 32lb long gun, 1 x 24lb long gun (both pivots), 2 x 9lb long guns |
| Launched | 1810, Oswego, New York; purchased 1812 |

Civilian *Charles & Ann*. Sold May 1815.

### Raven

| | |
|---|---|
| Displacement | 50 tons |
| Complement | 52 |
| Armament | 1 x mortar |
| Launched | 1810, Oswego, New York; purchased 1813 |

Civilian *Mary*. Fitted as a bomb vessel, but used as a transport. Sold May 1815.

### Julia

| | |
|---|---|
| Displacement | 82 tons |
| Complement | 35 |
| Armament | 1 x 32lb long gun, 1 x 12lb long gun (both pivots) |
| Launched | 1811, Oswego, New York; purchased 1812 |

Captured by British on August 10, 1813. Renamed *Confiance* by British and used as a transport. Recaptured October 1813 and sold 1814.

### Scourge

| | |
|---|---|
| Displacement | 110 tons |
| Complement | 66 |
| Armament | 4 x 6lb long guns, 6 x 4lb long guns |
| Launched | 1811, Niagara, New York; purchased 1812 |

British merchant *Lord Nelson*. Seized in June 1812 and purchased into US Navy. Sank in a squall off Twelve Mile Creek, August 8, 1813.

# Lake Erie and Upper Lakes
## Warships constructed by Great Britain

### *General Hunter* (brig-of-war)

| | |
|---|---|
| Dimensions | LBP: 61ft / Breadth: 18ft / Depth of Hold: 8ft / Draft: 8ft 6in |
| Displacement | 93 tons |
| Complement | 45 |
| Armament | 2 x 12lb carronades, 2 x 6lb long guns, 4 x 4lb long guns, 2 x 2lb long guns |
| Built | 1809, Amherstburg, Upper Canada |
| Entered Service | 1809, Provincial Marine |

Originally built as a schooner and altered to a brig prior to June 1812. Captured at Battle of Lake Erie, September 10, 1813. Sold 1815.

### *Queen Charlotte* (ship-rigged sloop-of-war)

| | |
|---|---|
| Dimensions | LBP: 92ft 6in / Breadth: 26ft / Depth of Hold: 11ft / Draft: 12ft |
| Displacement | 254 tons |
| Complement | 126 |
| Armament | 1812: 16 x 24lb carronades, 4 x 12lb long guns<br>1813: 14 x 24lb carronades, 1 x 24lb long gun (pivot), 2 x 24lb long guns |
| Built | 1810, Amherstburg, Upper Canada |
| Entered Service | 1810, Provincial Marine |

Served on upper lakes. Captured at Battle of Lake Erie, September 10, 1813. Laid up after capture. Sold 1825.

### *Lady Prevost* (armed schooner)

| | |
|---|---|
| Dimensions | LBP: 68ft / Breadth: 18ft 6in / Depth of Hold: 8ft / Draft: 9ft 6in |
| Displacement | 230 tons |
| Complement | 86 |
| Armament | 10 x 12lb carronades, 1 x 9lb long gun (pivot), 2 x 6lb long guns |
| Built | 1812, Amherstburg, Upper Canada |
| Entered Service | 1812, Provincial Marine |

Captured at Battle of Lake Erie, September 10, 1813. Commissioned as USS *Lady Prevost* afterwards. Sold 1815.

### *Detroit* (ship-rigged sloop-of-war)

| | |
|---|---|
| Dimensions | LBP: 92ft 6in / Breadth: 26ft / Depth of Hold: 11ft / Draft: 12ft |
| Displacement | 305 tons |
| Complement | 150 |
| Armament | 1 x 24lb carronade, 2 x 24lb long guns, 1 x 18lb long gun (pivot), 6 x 12lb long guns, 8 x 9lb long guns |
| Built | 1813, Amherstburg, Upper Canada |
| Entered Service | 1813, Royal Navy |

Design believed based on *Cruizer*-class sloop-of-war. Captured at Lake Erie, September 10, 1813. Sunk for preservation at Erie in 1815. Refloated in 1833, sold into merchant service. Wrecked in 1841 when an attempt was made to send it over Niagara Falls as a "spectacle." It grounded before reaching the falls, and sank.

## Vessels purchased by Great Britain

### *Little Belt* (sloop)

| | |
|---|---|
| Displacement | 90 tons |
| Complement | 20 |
| Armament | 1 x 12lb long gun (pivot), 2 x 6lb long guns |
| Launched | 1810, Black Rock, New York; purchased 1812 |

Civilian *Friends' Good Will*. Captured by British in 1812 at Mackinac. Captured at Battle of Lake Erie, September 10, 1813. Transport in American service. Trapped at Buffalo, New York, and burned to prevent capture by British in December 1813.

Daniel Dobbins chose Presque Isle as the location for the US Navy's shipyard on Lake Erie. Two major considerations driving the choice were the site's defensibility (a sand bar prevented British warships from approaching) and reasonable access to Pittsburgh. (AC)

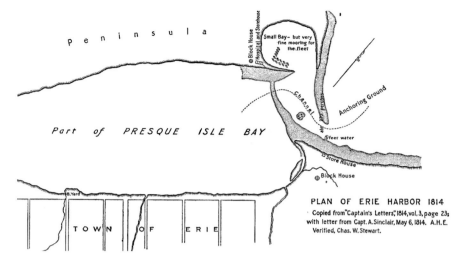

PLAN OF ERIE HARBOR 1814
Copied from "Captain's Letters", 1814, vol. 3, page 23; with letter from Capt. A. Sinclair, May 6, 1814. A.H.E. Verified, Chas. W. Stewart.

### Chippewa (schooner)

| | |
|---|---|
| Displacement | 70 tons |
| Complement | 20 |
| Armament | 1 x 9lb long gun (pivot) |
| Launched | 1811, Maumee River, Michigan Territory; purchased 1812 |

Captured by British in 1812. Re-captured at Battle of Lake Erie, September 10, 1813. Used as a transport by the Americans. Burned to prevent capture by the British in December 1814 at Buffalo, New York.

### Erie (sloop)

| | |
|---|---|
| Displacement | 60 tons |
| Complement | 20 |
| Armament | 2 x 12lb long guns (1 pivot-mounted) |
| Launched | 1810 Black Rock, New York; purchased 1813 |

Captured by British in 1812 at Mackinac. Disposed of after July 1813, fate unknown.

## G   ONEIDA (BRIG-OF-WAR)

Dimensions: LBP: 85ft 6in / Breadth: 23ft 6in / Depth of Hold: 8ft / Draft: 10ft
Displacement: 262 tons
Complement: 150
Armament: 16 x 24lb carronades, 2 x 6lb long guns
Laid Down: 1809, Oswego, New York
Launched: March 31, 1809
Commissioned: 1809, US Navy

Construction of *Oneida* was authorized in 1807 to enforce Jefferson's Embargo Act. *Oneida* was intended as a gunboat, with one large gun on a bow-mounted pivot, but its builder Henry Eckford modified it into a more seaworthy brig-rigged vessel. The 32lb long gun intended for use on *Oneida* was never mounted, and was used instead as a shore gun. Two carriage-mounted 6lb long guns substituted as bow chasers. Eckford's design yielded hull lines more similar to ocean-going vessels than lakes vessels, and it had relatively little deadrise.

The first American warship on Lake Ontario, when launched *Oneida* was the most powerful warship on that lake. It triggered a lakes arms race, prompting the Provincial Marine to authorize construction of *Royal George* and *Prince Regent*.

While *Oneida* was swift when new, by 1812 its hull was foul, and it proved a sluggish sailer until refitted. *Oneida* acted as Chauncey's flagship in 1812, but as new and larger ships were built it played an increasingly secondary role. Sold in June 1815, the navy subsequently repurchased it, and placed it in ordinary at Sackett's Harbor. Sold again in 1825, and served on Lake Ontario as a merchant vessel until 1837.

## Warships constructed by the United States

Both sides converted existing merchant vessels for use in their fleets. Solid bulwarks were added and guns mounted – often on pivots – on the upper deck. This is USS *Somers*, as it was thought to appear at the Battle of Lake Erie. (LOC)

### *Adams* (brig-of-war)

| | |
|---|---|
| Displacement | 125 tons |
| Complement | Unknown – approx 60 |
| Armament | 6 x 6lb long guns |
| Built | 1801, River Rogue, Michigan Territory |
| Entered Service | 1801, US Army |

Captured by British in 1812 at Mackinac. Disposed of after July 1813, fate unknown.

### *Porcupine, Tigress* (armed schooners)

| | |
|---|---|
| Dimensions | LBP: 60ft 6in / Breadth: 17ft 9in / Draft: 5ft 3in |
| Displacement | 52 tons |
| Complement | 25–35 |
| Armament | 1 x 32lb long gun (pivot) |
| Built | 1813, Erie, Pennsylvania |
| Entered Service | 1813, US Navy |

Built by Daniel Dobbins. *Tigress* captured on September 3, 1814. Served as HMS *Confiance*. Laid up after the war, it sank at its moorings during 1820s. *Porcupine* laid up in 1815. Turned over to revenue service in 1819. Returned to US Navy in 1821. Sold 1825; merchant vessel until 1873

### *Scorpion* (armed schooner)

| | |
|---|---|
| Dimensions | LBP: 68ft 6in / Breadth: 18ft 6in / Draft: 5ft 6in |
| Displacement | 663 tons |
| Complement | 35 |
| Armament | 1 x 24lb carronade, 1 x 32lb long gun (both pivots) |
| Built | 1813, Erie, Pennsylvania |
| Entered Service | 1813, US Navy |

Built by Adam and Noah Brown. Captured by British on September 3, 1814. Served in Royal Navy as *Surprise*. Laid up post-war. Sank at its moorings in 1820s.

### *Ariel* (armed schooner)

| | |
|---|---|
| Displacement | 75 tons |
| Complement | 36 |
| Armament | 4 x 12lb long guns |
| Built | 1813, Erie, Pennsylvania |
| Entered Service | 1813, US Navy |

Built by Adam and Noah Brown. Trapped at Buffalo, NY in December 1813, and burned to prevent capture by British.

### *Lawrence, Niagara* (brigs-of-war)

(see plate A)

## Vessels purchased by the United States

### *Trippe* (sloop)

| | |
|---|---|
| Displacement | 60 tons |
| Complement | 35 |
| Armament | 1 x 24lb long gun (pivot) |
| Built | 1803, Black Rock, New York; purchased 1812 |

Civilian *Contractor*. Burned by British near Buffalo, New York, in 1813.

### Caledonia (brig)

| | |
|---|---|
| Displacement | 86 tons |
| Complement | 53 |
| Armament | 1 x 32lb carronade, 2 x 12lb long guns (all pivot) |
| Built | 1807, Amherstburg, Upper Canada; purchased 1813 |

Built for Canadian North West Company, and captured at Fort Erie. Purchased February 6, 1813. Sold in May 1815; renamed *General Wayne* on merchant service. Reportedly sank in Lake Erie in the 1830s.

### Somers (schooner)

| | |
|---|---|
| Displacement | 65 tons |
| Complement | 30 |
| Armament | 1 x 32lb carronade, 1 x 24lb long gun (both pivots) |
| Built | 1809, Black Rock, New York; purchased 1812 |

Civilian *Catherine*. Captured by British on August 12, 1814 on Lake Huron. Sunk as blockship in 1814. Raised 1815; renamed HMS *Huron*. Sank at moorings prior to 1825.

### Ohio (schooner)

| | |
|---|---|
| Displacement | 87 tons |
| Complement | 20 |
| Armament | 1 x 9lb long gun (pivot) |
| Built | 1810, Cleveland, Ohio, Purchased 1812 |

Captured by British on August 12, 1814 on Lake Huron. Sunk as blockship 1814. Raised 1815, renamed HMS *Sauk*. Sank at moorings prior to 1825.

## Lake Champlain
## Warships constructed by Great Britain

### Linnet (brig-of-war)

| | |
|---|---|
| Dimensions | LBP: 82ft 6in / Breadth: 27ft / Depth of Hold: 6ft 8in / Draft: 8ft 6in |
| Displacement | 260 tons |
| Complement | 125 |
| Armament | 16 x 12lb long guns |
| Built | 1814, Isle aux Noix, Quebec |
| Entered Service | 1814, Royal Navy |

Built by William Simons; renamed from *Niagara* to *Linnet* during construction. Captured at Plattsburg, September 11, 1814. Taken into US Navy. Laid up in 1814, and dismantled in 1815. Ordered sold in 1825; sank at moorings after no buyers appeared.

### Confiance

| | |
|---|---|
| Dimensions | LBP: 47ft 5in / Breadth: 37ft 2in / Draft: 7ft |
| Displacement | 1,200 tons |
| Complement | 325 |
| Armament | 4 x 32lb carronades, 6 x 24lb carronades, 27 x 24lb long guns (1 pivot mounted) |
| Built | 1814, Isle aux Noix, Quebec |
| Entered Service | 1814, Royal Navy |

Built by William Simons. Captured at Plattsburg on September 11, 1814. Taken into US Navy. Laid up in 1814. Sank at moorings in 1820; sold to salvagers in 1825.

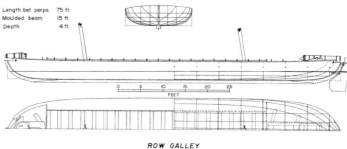

*ROW GALLEY*

**ABOVE**

This painting of the battle fought between the fleets commanded by Chauncey and Yeo on August 10, 1813, was painted by Midshipman Peter Spicer. He served on *Oneida* (the brig at the extreme right, backing its sails) during this battle. (USNH&HC)

**ABOVE RIGHT**

Gunboats were small warships armed with one or two large guns, intended to be rowed in battle. Used by both sides to protect harbors, rivers, or sheltered waters, these flat-bottomed vessels were impractical on coastal waters, but useful on the lakes, especially at Lake Champlain. (Courtesy of Kevin Crisman)

## Warships constructed by the United States

| *Saratoga* (ship-rigged sloop-of-war) | |
| --- | --- |
| Dimensions | LBP: 143ft 6in / Breadth: 36ft 4in / Draft: 12ft 6in |
| Displacement | 734 tons |
| Complement | 212 |
| Armament | 6 x 42lb carronades, 12 x 32lb carronades, 8 x 24lb long guns |
| Built | 1814, Vergennes, Vermont |
| Entered Service | 1814, US Navy |

Designed and built by Noah and Adam Brown, and completed in 2½ months. American flagship at Plattsburg. Laid up in 1814. Sank at moorings in 1821; sold to salvagers in 1825.

| *Ticonderoga* (schooner-rigged sloop-of-war) | |
| --- | --- |
| Dimensions | LBP: 120ft / Breadth: 25ft / Draft: 12ft 6in |
| Displacement | 375 tons |
| Complement | 112 |
| Armament | 3 x 32lb carronades, 4 x 18lb long guns, 10 x 12lb long guns |
| Built | 1814, Vergennes, Vermont |
| Entered Service | 1814, US Navy |

Converted from a Lake Champlain merchant steamboat into a sailing warship while under construction. Laid up in 1814. Sank at moorings prior to 1825; sold to salvagers in 1825.

| *Surprise/Eagle* (brig-of-war) | |
| --- | --- |
| Dimensions | LBP: 117ft 3in / Breadth: 34ft 9in / Draft: 11ft 6in |
| Displacement | 500 tons |
| Complement | 150 |
| Armament | 12 x 32lb carronades, 8 x 18lb long guns |
| Built | 1814, Vergennes, Vermont |
| Entered Service | 1814, US Navy |

Designed and built by Noah and Adam Brown, and completed in 31 days. Named *Surprise* by its captain, renamed *Eagle* by MacDonough. Laid up in 1814. Sank at moorings prior to 1825; sold to salvagers in 1825.

## Sloops purchased by the United States

| *President* | |
| --- | --- |
| Displacement | 80 tons |
| Armament | 6 x 18lb columbiads, 6 x 12lb long guns |
| Launched | Date and place unknown; purchased 1812 |

Transport in 1814, when captured. Renamed HMS *Icicle*. Sold in 1815.

| Eagle | |
|---|---|
| Displacement | 110 tons |
| Complement | 50 |
| Armament | 7 x 18lb carronades, 4 x 6lb long guns |
| Launched | Date and place unknown; purchased 1812 |

Civilian *Bull Dog*. Captured by British on June 3, 1813, near Isle aux Noix. Taken into Royal Navy as *Shannon*. Renamed *Chub* 1814. Captured at Plattsburg on September, 11 1814. Sold by Americans in 1815.

| Growler | |
|---|---|
| Displacement | 112 tons |
| Complement | 50 |
| Armament | 10 x 18lb carronades, 1 x 6lb long guns |
| Launched | Date and place unknown; purchased 1812 |

Civilian *Hunter*. Captured by British on June 3, 1813, near Ile aux Noix. Taken into Royal Navy as *Broke*. Renamed *Finch* 1814. Captured at Plattsburg on September 11, 1814. Sold by Americans in 1815.

| Preble | |
|---|---|
| Displacement | 80 tons |
| Complement | 50 |
| Armament | 2 x 18lb carronades, 7 x 12lb long guns |
| Launched | Date and place unknown; purchased 1813 at Plattsburg |

Sold 1815.

| Montgomery | |
|---|---|
| Armament | 2 x 18lb columbiads, 9 x 9lb long guns |
| Launched | Date and place unknown; purchased 1813 |

Used as transport 1814. Sold 1815.

| Wasp | |
|---|---|
| Armament | 2 x 12 lb guns |
| Launched | Date and place unknown; purchased 1813 |

Disposed of prior to 1815, fate unknown.

# GLOSSARY

**Brig:** A two-masted square-rigged ship with a foremast and mainmast.

**Brig-rigged:** A ship with a foremast and a mainmast, carrying square sails, is said to be brig-rigged.

**Carronade:** A short-barreled smoothbore gun designed to throw much heavier balls than a traditional long gun. A 12lb carronade weighed less than a 4lb long gun, but could fire a ball that weighed three times as much. It threw its shot a shorter range than a long gun firing the equivalent shot, however.

**Deadrise:** The angle of the hull upward from horizontal as measured at the widest frame of a ship.

**Fore-and-aft sails:** Triangular and trapezoidal sails that were rigged parallel to the length of the ship. The sails set on the stays that supported the masts were called staysails or jibsails (if they were on the jib stays). The sail set on a gaff and boom attached behind the mizzenmast was called the gaff, spanker or spencer sail, depending on the navy, period, and rig. Fore-and-aft sails were used to help steer the ship, and when beating into the wind.

**Forecastle:** A raised platform at the front of a ship, generally used to manage the anchors and foremast and to provide protection from a head sea.

**Frigate:** A sailing warship with one full gun deck and additional guns mounted on the forecastle and quarterdeck. A warship with a full gun deck and additional guns mounted only on the quarterdeck is sometimes called a jackass frigate.

**Pivot:** A gun mounted so that the carriage holding the gun can rotate. This system allows the gun to be fired to either side of the deck.

**Quarterdeck:** A partial deck above the main deck or gun deck where the navigation and operation of the ship is managed. Generally the quarterdeck starts between the mainmast and the mizzenmast.

**Rake:** Firing a broadside down the length of the opposing warship, either into the stern or bow. Raking shot caused much more damage because it went the length, rather than the breadth, of a ship.

**Receiving Ship:** A ship used to temporarily house recruits or unassigned sailors until they can be permanently assigned to a ship.

**Schooner:** A ship with two or more masts rigged with fore-and-aft sails. A topsail-schooner had a square topsail on the foremast. A bald-headed schooner had only fore-and-aft sails.

**Ship-of-the-line:** A ship-rigged warship with at least two full gun decks and additional guns on the quarterdeck and forecastle that is strong enough to stand in the line of battle. Ships-of-the-line mounted 64 to 140 guns.

**Ship-rigged:** A ship with at least three masts, all carrying square sails, is said to be ship-rigged.

**Sloop:** A small, single-masted ship rigged with fore-and-aft sails.

**Sloop-of-war:** A warship with guns mounted only on the gun deck. Three-masted sloops-of-war are often called ship-sloops, and two-masted sloops-of-war are often called brig-sloops. Occasionally a sloop-of-war had additional guns mounted on the quarterdeck. These are also referred to as "post" ships or jackass frigates.

**Snow:** A type of brig, which had a trysail mast mounted immediately behind the mainmast on which the mizzen sail was mounted.

**Spar deck:** A flush deck on an American frigate consisting of the forecastle, quarterdeck, and the gangways connecting the quarterdeck and forecastle. Generally there is an opening amidships spanned by skids on which the spare spars and ship's boats are kept.

**Squaresail:** Four-sided sails, occasionally square, but more often trapezoidal, set on spars and perpendicular to the length of the ship. American frigates generally mounted five, and sometimes six, sails on their masts. From lowest to highest were the course, topsail, topgallant, royal, skysail, and moonsail or hope-in-heaven. (The name of the sixth sail varied widely.)

USS *Niagara* in Put-in-Bay for the centennial celebration of the Battle of Lake Erie, after it was restored in 1913. (LOC)

# BIBLIOGRAPHY

Canney, Donald L., *Sailing Warships of the US Navy*, US Naval Institute Press, Annapolis, MD (2001)

Chapelle, Howard I., *The History of the American Sailing Navy*, W.W. Norton, New York (1998)

Chapelle, Howard I., *The History of American Sailing Ships*, W.W. Norton, New York (1988)

Cooper, James Fenimore, *Ned Myers; Or, a Life Before the Mast*, Naval Institute Press, Annapolis, MD (1989)

Crisman, Kevin J., *The Eagle: An American Brig on Lake Champlain During the War of 1812*, New England Press, Shelburne, Vermont (1987)

Crisman, Kevin J., *The History and Construction of the United States Schooner Ticonderoga*, Eyrie Publications (1987)

Cruikshank, Ernest (ed.), *The Documentary History Of The Campaign On The Niagara Frontier*, 9 vols, Lundy's Lane Historical Society, Welland, Ontario (1896–1908)

Dudley, William S. (ed.), *The Naval War of 1812, A Documentary History*, 3 vols, Naval Historical Center, Department of the Navy, Washington, DC (1965)

Emery, Eric B., *The Last of Mr. Brown's Mosquito Fleet: A History of the American Row Galley Allen on Lake Champlain, 1814–1825*, Doctorial Thesis, Texas A&M University (2003)

Gordon, Leeanne E., *Newash And Tecumseth: Analysis Of Two Post-War Of 1812 Vessels On The Great Lakes*, Master's Thesis, Texas A&M University (2009)

Harland, John, *Seamanship in the Age of Sail*, Naval Institute Press, Annapolis, MD (1990)

Mahan, Alfred T., *Sea Power In Its Relations To The War Of 1812*, 2 vols, S. Low, Marston & Co., London (1905)

Malcomson, Robert, *Warships of the Great Lakes 1754–1834*, Naval Institute Press, Annapolis, MD (2001)

Mooney, James L. (ed.), *The Dictionary of American Naval Fighting Ships*, US Government Printing Office, Washington, DC (1977)

Roosevelt, Theodore, *The Naval War of 1812*, G.P. Putnam's Sons, New York and London (1900)

Sabick, Christopher R., *His Majesty's Hired Transport Schooner Nancy*, Master's Thesis, Texas A&M University (2004)

Walker, Daniel R., *The Identity And Construction Of Wreck Baker, A War Of 1812 Era Royal Navy Frigate*, Master's Thesis, Texas A&M University (2006)

Washburn, Erika, *Linnet: The History and Archaeology of a Brig from the War of 1812*, Master's Thesis, Texas A&M University (1998)

Winfield, Rif, *British Warships In The Age Of Sail 1793–1817: Design, Construction, Careers and Fates*, Seaforth Publishing (2008)

After the War of 1812, Henry Eckford went on to a long career as a naval shipbuilder. Among the projects he built for the US Navy was the ship-of-the-line *Ohio*, shown here. It was considered the finest ship-of-the-line in the US Navy. (LOC)

THE PORT OF BUFFALO IN 1813.

**BELOW LEFT**
A romanticized view of the construction of the American fleet at Presque Isle. It does, however, accurately capture the primitive conditions of many lakes shipyards, especially those on Lake Erie and Lake Champlain (AC)

**BELOW RIGHT**
While secondary to Erie, Pennsylvania, for naval purposes during the War of 1812, Buffalo, New York, was the most important commercial port on the lake, and subject to British raids. One such raid in December 1813 led to the destruction of four US Navy schooners. (AC)

# INDEX

Figures in **bold** refer to illustrations.